An unplugged Kitchen

An unplugged Kitchen

An unplugged Kitchen

An Unplugged Kitchen

An unplugged Kitchen

the unplugged Kitchen

An Unplugged Kitchen

An unplugged Kitchen

the unplugged Kitchen

Unplugged Kitchen

also by Viana La Place

VERDURA

PANINI, BRUSCHETTA, CROSTINI

co-author

CUCINA FRESCA

PASTA FRESCA

CUCINA RUSTICA

VIANA LA PLACE

unplugged

kitchen

a return to the simple, authentic joys of cooking

PHOTOGRAPHS BY MARIA ROBLEDO   ILLUSTRATIONS BY ANN FIELD

William Morrow and Company, Inc.
New York

Copyright © 1996 by Viana La Place
Illustrations copyright © 1996 by Ann Field
Photographs copyright © 1996 by Maria Robledo

It is the policy of William Morrow and Company, Inc., and its imprints and affiliates, recognizing the importance of preserving what has been written, to print the books we publish on acid-free paper, and we exert our best efforts to that end.

Library of Congress Cataloging-in-Publication Data

La Place, Viana.
    Unplugged kitchen : a return to the simple, authentic joys of cooking / by Viana La Place.
       p. cm.
    Includes index.
    ISBN 0-688-11313-3
    1. Cookery, Italian.   I. Title.
TX723.L23   1996
641.5945—dc20   96-12631
                                                                                                          CIP

Printed in the United States of America

First Edition

1 2 3 4 5 6 7 8 9 10

BOOK DESIGN BY PH.D

To Jim K, who never ceases to amaze me.

Message of Thanks

I feel inordinately lucky in my work to be surrounded by people I hugely respect and admire. I'm honored to consider them my friends.

Since my first days as a cookbook author, I have been blessed with an extraordinary editor—supportive, warm and giving, insightful, and, very important, a kindred spirit. To Ann Bramson, I owe an enormous debt of gratitude for believing in me enough to allow me to find my voice, and then letting me express it.

Since day one, I've benefited from the encouragement and guidance of my agents, Maureen and Eric Lasher. To say that they are always there for me is an understatement. I rely on them. When I call I know I will find a thoughtful opinion and sound advice, along with an equal measure of sweetness and kindness.

To Clive Piercy, art director; Maria Robledo, photographer; and Ann Field, illustrator, I owe the profoundly beautiful look and feel of this book. They have brilliantly conveyed its message, its essence, through color and line, light and shadow. Their passion and conviction infuse every page—and to them I am forever grateful.

Without the love of a family, work would weigh heavier, joys might be less joyful. I am forever indebted to my mother—she has been my model and inspiration since my very youngest days. To the memory of my father—his rigorous intellect and analytical mind, his visionary thinking, his kindness, guide me every day. My sisters, Maria and Michelle, enrich my life in so many ways. They have encouraged me when I grew weary, and cheered me on when the task of writing this book seemed overwhelming. And to the memory of my grandmothers, Caterina and Damiana—who touched me deeply with the stories of their lives, and fed me with their dishes that tasted like love.

From the deepest part of my heart, I thank you one and all.

Contents

The Journey

I've worked on this book for the past four years. During this time, I've experienced all the trials and tribulations, and all the joy, that life offers.

There have been family illnesses, one a brush with death, and recovery; fluctuating finances; three geographical changes, one of which was major and changed my life for the better. Over this time I've lived in the country, in the city, and I'm now in an urban setting that, to my eyes, resembles paradise. And I've cooked for this book in three very different kitchens.

In the course of cooking and writing, I've turned to friends and colleagues for comfort or some friendly advice, or when I wanted to share an afternoon at a sidewalk café watching the world go by.

Writing this cookbook has been a personal journey for me. In a sense I've stripped myself bare in these pages, by presenting food I love without any barriers or filters, and sharing with you my life, growing up in southern California but also within the bosom of an Italian family—living a life that is close to that experienced every day in Italy.

For me, as a first-generation American with my born-raised-educated-and-married-in-Italy parents, my sisters, and my Italian grandmothers, inside our house it was always Italy, even though we were geographically located in the heart of emerging suburbia.

If you closed your eyes and deeply inhaled the scent of pasta sauce cooking on a Sunday afternoon, or tasted the salad of green beans, tomato, and potato pungent with vinegar, or noticed the marble-topped tables and bouquets of garden flowers in our fifties suburban living room, or listened to the voluble, melodic (and sometimes operatic!) sounds of Italian being spoken, you would swear you were in Italy.

But outside our house—at school, at the local shopping center, at the drive-through hamburger stand, with my friends at the movies, in the school cafeteria—I was part of American culture.

In this book my desire has been to show this duality in my life as translated and transmuted through food. And to present a style of cooking that closely reflects how I ate while growing up, and how I eat now. This approach looks to nature, in all its astounding variety, and its infinite power to nurture and delight, as its guiding star.

The recipes presented in this book are based on my deeply held belief that the food, as well as the style of cooking and eating, of Italy is an exquisite paradigm for a way of eating that we can all embrace.

This mode of cooking need not be bound by Italian ingredients but can encompass those from outside Italy's physical boundaries. In these pages, I've tried to take the full range of the raw materials I love and value and to refract them through the prism of my own experiences, to reflect a supremely wholesome, humane, and life-affirming style of eating. This has been not only my goal, but my driving passion.

In the following pages, Italy is never very far away. There is much that I've come to understand about Italian food through living and loving what it has to offer, and from listening to and learning all that it has to teach.

America is in these pages, too: California in the twenties, America at the turn of the twentieth century, America at the turn of the twenty-first century. A friend in beautiful, mystical Ojai who lives among the citrus groves. Also the backyard of my childhood home in southern California . . . and the terrace of my new home in San Francisco.

But America is only part of the story, albeit a significant one. China is here. And Lebanon. And Spain. And a friend from Jordan.

Here, you'll find my opinions (some stated quite strongly) about food, as well as beliefs that have taken shape over the many years in which food and its wider implications, both local and global, have been integral to my life.

I've included technical advice, childhood memories, adventures recalled, discussion of kitchen tools, food tips and guides, and a running commentary, such as the "Don't Throw It Away!" guides interspersed throughout the book.

This book is both a condensation of a wide range of thoughts on various related topics—cooking, gardens, food, nature, kitchens, and culture—and an opening up and expansion. I've opened up my heart to reveal my unexpurgated feelings about food processors; to offer recipes for the seemingly rough, almost rudimentary food I almost always prefer to cook at home; and to share my most private emotions when I hold a tangerine to my nose in winter to breathe in its scent.

I hope the personal transcends the I, to embrace everyone—since it is only when we are at our most honest that we truly feel the joy and liberation that comes with the universal.

Using this book / rites and rituals.

7.

can cooking be codified?

Cooking is a living, breathing act that defies codification or regimentation. One peach may be as sweet as nectar, another less so. My salt may be saltier than your salt.

The act of cooking always contains elements of surprise—it is changeable and variable, like all that comes from nature. Think of how a rose in bloom changes every day. How clouds move and change shape.

Cooking, above all, requires responsiveness and being in the moment.

measurements

Sometimes, with all the measuring devices and temperature gauges and stainless steel equipment in modern kitchens, it seems more appropriate to don a white laboratory coat to cook, as was done in the early "test" kitchens when measurements became codified in the way we know them today.

Carefully calibrated measuring spoons and cups turn what should be a casual, intuitive process into one that is clinical and scientific. After all, a tablespoon is a large spoon that is used at the *table* for eating; a teaspoon is one that is used to stir *tea* or coffee. A measuring cup is the size of a *teacup* or coffee cup.

I suggest using spoons that you use daily for eating and a good old coffee cup for measuring ingredients. A large soup spoon equates to a tablespoon, and teaspoons are all basically the same size; for amounts smaller than a teaspoon, just cast a steady eye and make your best estimate.

I don't recommend this approach if you plan to make elaborate desserts that require exactitude; in this case, it is much more reliable to depend on precise measurements. On the other hand, I do suggest that you use this less rigid way of measuring when you make bread at home—after all, it is a matter of feel. No harm will ever befall you if you use this informal method of measuring—a bit more or less olive oil, water, herbs, and so forth will never jeopardize the results of your efforts.

After weaning yourself from formal measurements, it will be easier to take the next step—cooking without the need for measuring devices. Feel and smell and sight will become your touchstones. Your hand will be the measure for flour; a pinch of salt from a saltcellar will represent a teaspoon; a larger pinch, a tablespoon; a puddle of olive oil poured into a sauté pan will equal three tablespoons. And that is what the process of cooking should be: natural, free-flowing, and heartfelt.

defining a style of eating

Many of us have been searching for a descriptive word to identify the new style of cooking and eating that we follow.

My own primary source of sustenance is from flora rather than fauna. My way of eating embraces all the world of plants, but also includes small amounts of fish and meat.

I've considered calling myself an herbivore, although I don't actually qualify. Right now, I'm toying with the idea of calling myself a "floran," from the word "flora," used to differentiate between the two types of life on earth—flora and fauna, plant life and animal life.

A floran eating style would include fish and meat, but in much smaller proportions in relation to fruits, vegetables, flowers, greens, grains, or beans. I find the term "vegetarian" is too restrictive and tends to conjure up the wrong associations. Being a floran sounds nicely poetic, and since it's a new term, it can stand for a new and different way to eat.

But then again, I'm not so sure we have to define the way we eat in the first place.

force of nature

The word "vegetable" has a much broader meaning than that normally assigned to it. It means, first and foremost, the plant world, any plant.

The first entry in the dictionary for the word is: of, or having the nature of, plants in general, the vegetable kingdom. Also: broadly, any plant, as distinguished from animal or inorganic matter. It is related to the words "vegetate," to grow as plants, and "vegetation," the act or process of vegetating as well as signifying plant life in general.

However, both vegetable and vegetating are also used pejoratively. If a person is described as being like a vegetable, it means he or she leads a drab, unthinking existence or, having lost consciousness, no longer has the use of his or her mind. Although the root words of vegetate include "lively," "to enliven," "to quicken and wake the senses," the dictionary states that vegetating means to exist with little mental or physical activity, and to lead a dull and inactive life. But nature is a force. Not benign, not passive. Certainly not without physical activity.

Consider plants thrusting up through a city sidewalk, toward the heat of the sun, with a life force capable of cracking cement. Think of plants forcing themselves upward through hard-packed earth, through stone and rock, in an effort to thrive and flourish. They have an energy that is pulsating, active—sending out roots and feelers. If they are thirsty, they hungrily search for water. Plants can be fierce; wild growth can strangle and kill other plants.

But plants are more than just rapacious green monsters. They possess a delicacy of form and color that defies describing it with any justice. A plant unfurls a delicate, trembling leaf that is as intricately veined as a human hand. A tightly enclosed rosebud opens slowly to reveal a million petals, each petal shaded from white peach to yellow daffodil to russet red to black. A peapod sends out shoots and lacy tendrils as its hidden green pearls swell with sweet juices.

Vegetables have a life all their own—a world different from ours, but no less vital, with a way of communicating that we are not privy to, perhaps to be revealed to us only in our dreams.

where flavors meet

I like to be able to *taste* what I'm eating; I guess you can say it's at the center of my philosophy of eating. I don't like flavors that are too mixed up or fused into foods.

I prefer to taste the flavors separately or, alternatively, taste the point at which the flavors, each distinct and alive, come together, the exciting edge where they merge.

In my book *panini, bruschetta, crostini,* in the preface to the recipe for Toasted Bittersweet Chocolate Panino, I discuss the point at which the flavors of chocolate and bread meet.

When I stir sugar and dark cocoa into my dessert ricotta, I stop short of blending them in uniformly, so that I can taste a bit of bitterness from the cocoa and a bit of pure sweetness from the sugar. This keeps my taste buds lively and prevents the flavors from becoming muddy, and more directly represents the true tastes contained within the dish.

When I make a salad dressing, I barely mix the oil, lemon, and sea salt with the greens and add each ingredient into the salad separately, so the flavors are fresh and untarnished when they come together—leaves, oil, lemon, salt.

Come with me where flavors meet!

eating well

Eating well doesn't mean consuming course after course of fancy food; it doesn't require exotic ingredients; nor does it necessarily mean drinking only vintage wines.

Eating well can be done in the sparest of settings. It doesn't require anything more than honest wine or sweet water. And the ingredients can be familiar and humble.

To eat well means to know how and when to eat; it means eating appropriately. It is an attitude of respect toward the food you eat. It requires focus, an opening up of the senses, an embracing of the moment.

restaurant cooking versus home cooking

Don't confuse restaurant food with food prepared at home. Restaurant food often relies on strong, aggressive flavorings, novel food pairings, or highly time-consuming and technique-driven dishes to excite and impress patrons quickly and win them over.

Given the assembly-line nature of most restaurant kitchens, especially larger ones, food can taste good and look dazzling but still leave one dissatisfied, since the experience is unavoidably impersonal.

In many countries around the world, home cooking is considered the paragon of good cooking. And to say that dishes served by a restaurant are as good as those prepared at home—by careful, loving hands, in small quantities to feed one family—is the highest compliment one can pay.

At home food need not fulfill any other function than to nourish and sustain. But simple foods require the greatest attention and care to be truly good. And that is the nature of home cooking.

on arranging and garnishing food

Food should not be designed, it should be natural. Beautiful food is food that comes as close as possible to its natural state, that reflects the changing seasons.

you are now entering the twilight zone

I always feel I've entered the twilight zone when shopping in supermarkets. Produce is always available, but in pale versions that look as if they had grown under a rock; more foods are sold in boxes, plastic containers, and cans than are sold fresh; the frozen-food section keeps getting bigger and bigger, and it's so incredibly cold there that I wish I'd worn my winter coat and gloves.

The cheese section emits no fragrance, with shrink-wrapped cheeses all in a row. The fish is questionable, the meat is suspect; horror stories abound of fish and meat being doctored to hide the smells of putrefaction. And where are all the enticing smells of ripe fruits and vegetables? The deep, yeasty aroma of slow-rising hearth-baked breads? This is real sensory deprivation.

Inside the market I lose my sense of time. Is it day or night? It's like being in Las Vegas, where clocks don't exist. Sealed into the piped-in-air-and-artificially lighted environment, people look like characters out of *The Night of the Living Dead*. Mindless music goes round and round in your brain, and the scent of detergent is all-pervasive. You lose touch with nature and its role in keeping us alive.

15.

My best advice is to shop outside supermarkets as often as possible. It may take a bit of effort at first, but as you gradually discover small shops, ethnic markets, roadside stands, where pride is taken in the product and real human interaction takes place, and where the perfumes of nature make you giddy with delight, you'll see how life-enhancing shopping for food can be.

artisans/food crafters

Artisanal food makers—bread bakers, pastry makers, cheese makers, and others—are specialists and have proper equipment and access to the freshest ingredients.

Food artisans craft their wares in a special, artful way. Their foods are made in small batches by skilled hands. Artisans bring a tremendous amount of learning and experience to their craft, made manifest in each loaf of bread or each round of cheese. Their works are the product of passion and pride, not just commerce.

True artisanal foods reveal the hand of the maker, since they are crafted in a uniquely individual way. For example, a baker may bake black olive loaves, but each one will vary a bit in size or shape, be a bit bumpier from the dispersal of olives, or be less than perfectly rounded—a sign that human hands have been at work.

This touch of life is what makes the loaf of bread, the round of cheese eloquent and expressive—attributes that are unattainable in mass-produced foods.

a note about meat and poultry

Although I've never been a big meat eater, when I do eat meat I prefer to know where it comes from, if the animal has been fed healthy and wholesome foods, and how it's been treated.

It seems only fair to provide animals with a natural diet and a place to roam freely, and to give them the respect due all living creatures. This provides a better life for the animal, and meat that is more healthful to eat.

Since an animal's life was sacrificed in order to feed us, to me it is more respectful to eat only small portions of it. Let one animal feed many.

I think it's very important to support the humane treatment of animals—for it is a reflection of our own humanity. After all, if I were the source of food for other creatures, I would be grateful for a little kindness.

what's all the fuss about organic food?

I think it is important to remind ourselves that before World War II, almost all food was "organic." Organic food has been the norm since the beginnings of our cultivation of the earth.

Chemically treated foods, or more accurately, chemically tainted foods, have had only the briefest trial run on the planet. I and others of my generation, the so-called baby-boomer crowd, have been the guinea pigs.

It would seem only natural and right for us to question the use of these deadly chemicals and worry about the impact they will have on our bodies and on the earth.

Those in agribusiness and large chemical concerns may challenge the efficacy of natural methods of controlling pests; they may argue that nonorganic fertilizers must be used; they keep telling us that small amounts of chemicals do no harm; they claim that organic farming is impractical and too costly, and rush to tell us that we, the consumers, will suffer at the checkout counter. They may try to discredit growers and sellers of natural produce by saying the foods aren't really organic and that the public is being fooled and defrauded.

My question is, Who is really responsible for fooling and defrauding us? I say, the bottom line must be, "Is our food healthy or is it detrimental to our bodies and the body of the earth?"

Now that meat, poultry, and fish are stamped with advisory warning labels, why not, as has been suggested, also call for such labels to be placed on vegetables and fruits, on grains and beans, on herbs and spices when chemicals are applied in their production?

Organic food producers have formed groups to ensure that produce marked "organic" is indeed free of any contamination. These organizations scrupulously inspect produce and methods of agriculture to guarantee the claims. Organic growers take pride in the fruits of their labors and work hard to provide us with "clean food." They, more than anyone, want to eliminate poseurs and impostors.

Growers who are not as caring or as responsible should have to label *their* produce, and tell the truth about *their* product, right down to the chemically treated packing boxes.

I am lucky to live in an area where there is access to the produce of many organic farms—and I've used mostly organic ingredients when cooking for this book.

I'm happy to report that the move toward natural foods is not solely in California. It is a growing trend throughout our country, and in countries around the world as well.

Without having to look too far, you'll probably find organic growers in your area. Even if they are just a collection of backyard gardeners who trade back and forth, they represent an important and crucial step toward making our food safe and heightening awareness. And by supporting farmers who have made a commitment to us by farming in a natural way, prices will eventually become reasonable for everyone. That is the goal.

Then we can all trust the food we eat—know it is free of poisons, know it is grown with the seasons, know it has been given the benefit of full ripening and has been fed by the rich matter of the earth itself. And we can trust that no one will dim or diminish nature's gifts to us—the perfumes, flavors, and colors—profoundly complex, many shaded, intangible and fleeting, impossible to forget, impossible to define.

The unplugged Kitchen

21.

portrait of my kitchen

On sunny days the sun streams into my kitchen. Herbs in pots enjoy its warmth on the small terrace just outside the kitchen door. In the late afternoon, long, cool shadows start to fall across the green gardens below. On cloudy days I look out on gray, brooding skies and wind-whipped trees. I can step out on my terrace and watch the rain fall—smell the quickening scent of wet, black earth, feel the cool, moist air against my skin.

Work surfaces in my kitchen are worn and well used. There's my trusty chopping board; my grandmother's colander; my small cast-iron stovetop grill (which I bought in Italy many years ago); my heavy stone mortar and pestle—without it I'd be lost.

My kitchen isn't shiny and new; it is lived-in and soft-looking, with a high ceiling and tall windows. Old tiles, some chipped, line the counter; walls and cabinets are painted the color of white butter, covering layers of old paint, and there are traces of tomato-red trim peeking out from under palest yellow, a patina of other times and other lives lived in this kitchen. We eat at a very old, slightly creaky, wooden table.

Bunches of fresh bay leaves or spirals of lemon peel hang from the pot rack, depending on what I've been cooking or what I've gathered on my walks; plain mason jars are filled with beans, rice, sugar, stored in no particular order in the old pantry closet.

This kitchen suits my needs. It is a room I look forward to being in, not one to avoid; nor do I want to keep to a minimum the time I spend there. In this room I find comfort, adventure, a refuge in the sensual world—with scents and colors and tastes. It contains the memories of many good meals and some bad ones, lively conversation (sometimes too lively!), and of simple meals eaten alone in silent communion.

The kitchen is where I go to renew and refresh myself; it's the room I see first thing in the morning, or late at night when I can't sleep and crave a glass of sweet water. In this kitchen I've nursed myself back to health and comforted others who were tired or dispirited; laughed, fought, made plans, and shared dreams. It is the heart of the house, and if I listen carefully I can hear its heart beat.

The summer kitchen was in a long rear wing, and was built solidly of pine which time and weather had brought to a perfection of varied and lovely browns. There was a shallow passageway between the summer and winter kitchens, with cupboards for mops, brooms, brushes, and there, too, stood the wood boxes which it was my responsibility to keep full.

The door opening from this passage to the summer kitchen disclosed pine tables set under high windows, a sink with a green iron pump, a black iron range with a supplementary oil stove, and in the rear, a huge iron kettle set over a low brick stove for heating water for the weekly wash. A long lean-to porch with its back wall whitewashed, and furnished with a narrow wooden table and benches, ran along the western side of the summer kitchen, making a cool retreat where Stina prepared her vegetables in the morning.

Beyond the porch was a tar-paved court under the old pear tree, and there was the cistern and its wooden pump. White petunias and asters grew about the edge of this court, and shone like dim stars at night, attracting the night moths which hovered over them with quivering wings. In the warm summer afternoons hummingbirds hung like small suspended rainbows, and both day and night the perfume of the flowers drifted through the open windows into the house.

Stina (STINA)
Herman Smith, 1942

The summer kitchen of a Michigan farmhouse in the late 1800s that was the author's boyhood home

unplugging your kitchen

If you already own a food processor, consider leaving it in the cupboard. If you are thinking of buying one, I urge you not to.

I have never owned a food processor. This machine, so detrimental to good cooking, doesn't belong in home kitchens. Although I am well aware of the rush of modern life, I firmly believe most kitchen machines, although considered time-savers, in reality conspire to take up more of your time, since they must be assembled, disassembled, scraped out, cleaned, and generally fussed with.

By placing so much distance between yourself and the raw materials, no learning takes place. You never come to understand the process on a gut level. And you are deprived of the primal pleasures of preparing food.

It's like the difference between walking and driving. Driving may get you there faster, but walking opens you up to the scent of a flower, observation of the veining in a green leaf, the sheer joy of moving your body.

The processor separates you completely from the pleasures of physicality and from the sensual delight of working the food with your hands. The terrible noise it makes, that fierce whirring blade, the work bowl, the washing up—it's all so cumbersome and clumsy, and an assault on your senses. There is no grace or agility involved, no honing of your skills, no sense of peace and tranquillity.

Many of us suffer from mental stress as well as physical fatigue when we get home from work. And this trend will only increase with time and advances in technology.

A little pounding in the mortar might help you feel better and release some of the stresses of the day, not in an aggressive manner, but in a calming, rhythmical way. The color and scents will lift your spirits. And the small amount of actual muscle work involved will release tensions trapped in those muscles. What mentally seemed so hard and tiring will actually create energy.

You might even find that others want to join in and help out in the kitchen. After all, it's much more fun and rewarding to crush walnuts in a beautiful mortar with pestle firmly in hand than to experience the passivity inherent in watching a machine spin.

my unplugged kitchen

Here are the tools that I rely on when I cook, rather than resorting to a food processor. They've served me well over the years.

The important thing is to find comfort in the time you spend in the kitchen and to enjoy the physical aspects of cooking.

Kneading bread dough is a form of mild exercise as well as pure sensate pleasure: You can feel the dough, alive and metamorphosing, beneath your hands; bask in the rich, fecund smell of the yeast; see and feel the results of your efforts.

Soup put through a food mill is infinitely more interesting in texture than the dense pap that comes from processors. A few simple cranks of the mill handle will give you a light, finely textured soup.

Chopping and slicing by hand will result in more tender and flavorful foods, both when eaten raw and cooked, since the juices remain inside rather than being expelled by the speed and centrifugal force of the machine. Don't worry about getting those machine-perfect julienne strips. Who wants them anyway!

All of them are inexpensive, easy to use, lovely to look at, quiet, take just a moment to clean, and produce superior results. So, unplug your kitchen and enjoy the process.

1.

A few good knives. A chef's knife (a long one with a wide, curved blade) that is the right size and weight for you; an all-purpose utility knife (long and narrow); and a paring knife (small and narrow), invaluable for many tasks. And these knives need not be the most expensive to be effective.

2.

A large, heavy cutting board. Restaurant supply stores stock them at very reasonable prices. My cutting board measures $15 \times 20 \times 2$ inches.

3.

A hand-cranked cheese grater with a clamp attachment. With this simple, old-fashioned device, you can grate a mountain of cheese in moments. This type of grater is also excellent for grating nuts and bread. Efficient, quiet, a real workhorse in the kitchen. I bought mine many years ago in New York City's Little Italy.

4.

Several mortars and pestles in different sizes and weights, for grinding peppercorns, making pestos, crushing nuts. One large, heavy mortar with a generous bowl and a substantial wooden pestle is absolutely mandatory, especially if you harbor dreams of making pesto the real way. If you try to make pesto in a small mortar, you'll only meet with frustration and vow never to attempt it again.

Large, inexpensive stone mortars can be bought in Asian kitchen and hardware stores. One of my large mortars is from Thailand and cost just a little over $15. A real bargain!

5.

A simple hand-cranked food mill with three different disks (screens) for pureeing soups, removing seeds and peel from fresh tomatoes, and so forth.

6.

A Japanese slicer or mandoline with a hand protector for creating paper-thin slices of vegetables and cheeses (good for making vegetable carpaccios, see pages 54 and 56). This tool is not absolutely necessary, since you can use a vegetable peeler or your trusty knife to achieve similar results.

more unplugged kitchen companions

My kitchen contains other tools I've gathered over the years, some sentimental objects, others simply practical. I'm fond of them all and have loving feelings toward some of them. I admire their shapes, and the materials—wood, bamboo, terra-cotta; surfaces that are matte and glow softly; shiny objects that gleam in the sunlight.

Following is a list of more kitchen companions, and a little about their provenance. In a sense, they tell an abbreviated story of my life.

A zester

A stovetop hinged cast-iron grill I bought on an early trip to Rome and carried home in my suitcase—indispensable for easy and effective grilling on the stove

A heavyweight 12-inch sauté pan to make pasta sauces, sauté vegetables

A set of inexpensive serrated steak knives with green plastic handles, purchased in Bologna many years ago—very useful for all kinds of tasks

An assortment of gratin dishes. My favorites are Italian and made of glazed earthenware.

Tongs, as long as my arm, a holdover from my days in restaurant kitchens but a godsend in the home kitchen

A large, wood-topped, heavy-duty butcher-block table, 4 feet × 2 1/2 feet, about 1 3/4 inches thick, also from a restaurant supply house

A hand-cranked pasta machine

A small, hand-held one-sided cheese grater

A beautiful, elegant, large, heavy stainless-steel colander with sturdy feet and hard black plastic handles for a secure grip—a gift from Nonna, my mother's mother, which I cherish

A small, rickety aluminum colander, about fifty years old, that was my other grandmother's, which I treasure equally

Heavy potholders, not mitts

A large Chinese strainer with a bamboo handle and shallow wire-mesh bowl, 6 inches in diameter

A scale that measures ounces and pounds, capable of weighing up to 4³/4 pounds, also with
metric measurements

Mason-type jars in various sizes for storing bulk grains, beans, sea salt, sugar, and so forth

A Moka espresso pot—a simple stovetop coffee pot for making espresso, used on a daily
basis

Flat wooden spoons

Thin wooden skewers for piercing foods to test for doneness—long, skinny as a toothpick,
and strong

tea towels

The tea towels I use are an almost gauzy-thin white cotton. I buy them by the dozen
in hardware stores or kitchenware shops. They are a beautiful sight in my kitchen.

Tea towels are superior to heavier-weight kitchen towels and ones made of terry cloth in a
few, very important ways:

1.

Tea towels are fine and light as air, so they wash and dry more quickly and easily than thicker
dish towels. And dirt doesn't get imbedded in the fibers.

2.

Terry cloth often sheds, whereas tea towels have no long, loose fibers to get transferred to the
food.

3.

Tea towels are very large, at least four times the size of a conventional dish towel, so you can
gather the corners together to form a sack to shake dry big handfuls of rinsed lettuce. You can
use them to spread out masses of freshly washed basil for air-drying; or lay out row after row
of finished stuffed pasta shapes.

bye-bye to plastic wrap and paper towels

I've banished plastic wrap and paper towels from my cupboards. It was a difficult transition at first, but lately it's become easier.

Instead of plastic wrap, I suggest using wax paper, brown paper, and plates or upended bowls. I prefer the look and feel of sandwiches wrapped in wax paper or brown paper; an upended bowl on the counter efficiently traps the steam of roasted peppers being readied for peeling; a plate protects a bowl of soup in the refrigerator.

I avoid using paper towels in my kitchen. I have a strong suspicion that they are coated with strange chemicals to make them more absorbent. And they are incredibly wasteful of natural resources. Instead, I use clean cloth rags for kitchen spills, plain brown paper for absorbing the surface oil on fried foods, tea towels for draining excess water from salted tomato halves.

how to keep a clean kitchen

1.

Find a source for environmentally sound dishwashing lotion and a cleanser without chlorine and phosphates. If it's better for the environment, it's better for us.

2.

Buy good sponges, such as pop-up sponges, and change them frequently.

3.

Replace toxic cleaning products with safe ones. Your home, and especially your kitchen, is no place for toxic materials. Since most commercial cleaners give off fumes even when used in a well-ventilated room, they can cause all sorts of symptoms, from dizziness and headaches to feelings of disorientation. Certain chemicals found in spot removers, metal cleaners, and furniture polish can cause much more serious damage to your health.

4.

Use natural cleaning products, most of which are readily available (many are already in your cupboards) and inexpensive. Baking soda, white vinegar, olive oil, lemon juice, salt can all play a part in keeping your kitchen and the rest of your home clean.

It's time to replace that chemical smell that we've come to associate with cleanliness, and instead fill our kitchens and homes with clean natural scents, such as real lemon and dried lavender.

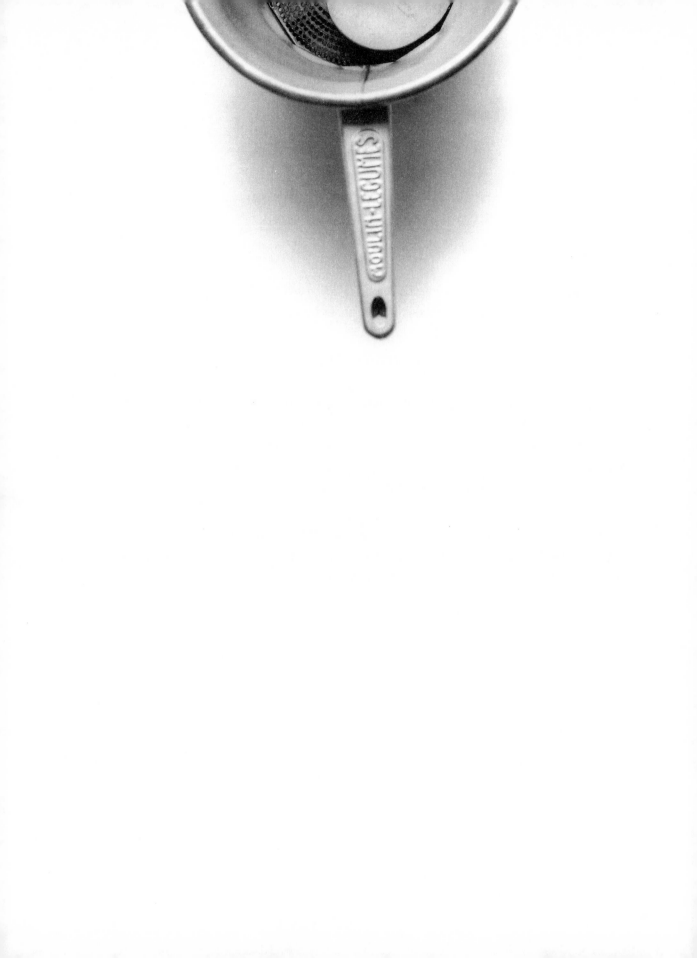

To begin

35.

(Begin)

on beginning a meal

I believe the food one eats before a meal should be simple, very fresh, and natural—unbelabored and unembellished, that requires no cooking or a bare minimum. I truly feel it is a more appropriate way to prepare for the meal that follows.

Excessive amounts of food served as appetizers before the main meal, cooked foods that inevitably lose some freshness and spontaneity, often just blunt and confuse, rather than stimulate, the appetite. A simple, uncomplicated dish allows the mind to focus quietly on flavor and texture, to gently awaken and arouse sensory awareness.

Antipasto means "before the meal." It shouldn't end up ruining the meal itself, by dulling one's excitement for what is to come.

The vision of the superabundant Italian antipasto table may have contributed to some mistaken notions. Remember that in Italy the heavily laden antipasto table is found only in restaurants. At home Italians eat a few olives or a sliver of cheese, or perhaps just some bread to take the edge off hunger and ready the stomach for the *pasto*, the meal, that is to come.

Although an antipasto table with an assortment of grilled, fried, marinated, and sliced foods looks stimulating to the eye, it often has the opposite effect on the palate. Rather than being a gentle prelude to the meal, it often stops the meal dead in its tracks. If you look at almost any culture, you will find that home-cooked meals start with pared-down offerings or nothing at all.

Most of the following dishes do not require cooking, and when they do, it is quite brief. Once you've done the groundwork—found a source for truly fresh-cut herbs, possibly grown your own French Breakfast radishes, located a market that stocks impeccably fresh raw nuts, restricted yourself once and for all to serving tomatoes only in summer—all that remains is to bask in the beauty and flavor of the food itself.

The way one begins a meal signals the spirit in which the food is offered. When everyone reaches into a communal basket of fresh herbs or dips bread into the same bowl of coarse, savory spread, a ritual, a *true* sharing of food takes place. How different this is from the isolation of separate plates and food placed before us.

toasted almonds

To appreciate how subtle and glorious simple toasted almonds can be, you must make them with carefully selected ingredients—new-crop almonds, sparkling sea salt, and exquisite almond oil.

I toast almonds in almond oil to amplify their aroma, so they more closely resemble sweet and highly fragrant Mediterranean almonds.

Buy nuts from a reputable vendor who can guarantee freshness. Old almonds lack essential oils, which impart flavor and scent. Ask for the Mission variety. Although not widely available, they are the most almondy-tasting around.

Almond oil is available in shops that stock a large variety of high-quality oils. It is definitely worth seeking out. Olive oil can also be used with excellent results.

2 cups raw, unpeeled almonds
Almond oil or extra-virgin olive oil
Fine sea salt | **MAKES 2 CUPS**

Immerse almonds in boiling water for 1 minute. Drain and pop off skins. Spread almonds on tea towel to dry.

Toss almonds in a little almond or olive oil until lightly moistened. Spread almonds out in a single layer on a baking sheet. Toast at 350° for about 15 minutes, or until colored a pale gold. Jerk baking sheet back and forth a few times to toast nuts evenly.

Spread hot almonds on a sheet of brown paper and sprinkle with salt. Let cool.

nuts, olives and

magical almonds

If you've only bought peeled and blanched almonds in plastic bags, you will never know how deliciously seductive almonds can be or how one can fall under their magic spell.

Almonds that are still tightly ensconced in their protective brown skin retain a greater amount of the essential oil that carries the magical flavor and perfume. If almonds are robbed of their skin for any but the briefest amount of time, the scent dissipates into the air and the flavor suffers as the oil evaporates.

For these very important reasons, please avoid buying blanched almonds, whole, sliced or slivered, no matter how tempted you might be. They have absolutely no flavor, and the texture is as dry as sawdust.

To keep raw almonds fresh, store them unpeeled in a tightly covered container in the freezer. To peel almonds, dip them in boiling water very briefly, about 1 minute, drain, and then pop the nut out of the loosened peel. Dry on tea towels.

potato chips.

Eating green almonds under a tree.

The first time I tasted green almonds I was nineteen years old and sitting under a big almond tree in a Sicilian garden. It was with surprise and pleasure that I cut through the protective green husks and tasted the crisp and moist, perfect white flesh of green almonds.

In almond-growing countries around the Mediterranean, almonds are eaten at all stages of ripeness. Early on, they are so tender that they can be eaten whole, green husk and all. Greeks like them sprinkled with sea salt and lemon juice.

When the husk begins to firm up, the nut is still soft enough to cut through with a knife, but not good for eating whole. The green husk is cut away, the almond peeled of its tender skin, and the juicy white almond meat is eaten—the way I enjoyed them in the Sicilian countryside. The French like to marinate green almonds at this stage in *vert jus*, the juice of not-quite-ripe green grapes.

In America green almonds are available in almond-growing regions in farmer's markets or specialty or ethnic food markets in late May and June.

green almonds

A few Mediterranean traditions combine to create a sublimely light and fresh-tasting beginning to a meal. Served outside under a shady tree, one could nibble on these tender, lovely white almonds forever. Lemony and herb-flecked, they go well with a cool glass of white wine.

If you're nowhere near an almond tree, don't despair. When raw almonds are soaked in spring water, they taste very much like green almonds.

6 dozen green almonds or raw, unpeeled almonds	A little finely chopped chervil or tarragon
Juice of 2 to 3 lemons, about 1/2 cup	
Fine sea salt	**MAKES 6 DOZEN**

If using dry raw almonds, drop almonds in boiling water for 1 minute. Drain. When cool enough to handle, pop off skins. Soak peeled almonds overnight in spring water to cover. Drain well.

With green almonds, use a paring knife and cut lengthwise all along the natural division of the green husk. Be careful not to cut through the almond itself. With the knife still inserted in the husk, pry open the two halves and free the almond. Don't worry if you split a few almonds in half. You'll soon master the technique.

To peel, first make a very small cut into the skin at the pointy end of the almond, then peel from pointy end down.

Place the almonds in a small bowl and cover with lemon juice. Drain after 1 hour, reserving the lemon juice for another use. Spread almonds on a tea towel and let drain briefly. Gently toss almonds with herb of choice and sea salt.

warm black olives

Heat causes flavors to expand and open up. Black olives have a wine-rich perfume, deep and resonant. A quick sauté of oil-cured black olives, cooked just enough to heat them through, helps unlock the full dimension of their flavor. You could add herbs or other flavors, but why not simply savor the true, pure olive flavor?

Take time to find a good source for exceptional black olives. What makes them good? Suave, moist, meaty flesh and deep, strong flavor, without excessive salt.

Oil-cured black olives, without added seasonings

Select a sauté pan large enough to contain the olives in one layer. Warm the olives over low heat, stirring often with a wooden spoon, for 3 to 4 minutes, or until the flesh is heated all the way through. Serve right away, with rustic bread.

don't throw it away.

It would be a sad loss to throw away the precious peels of citrus fruits.

When using organic citrus fruits, save the peels for candying. Or zest the rinds and add to salads, soups, pastas, rice dishes, and desserts.

Thick strips of air-dried peel can be used to scent rooms. For linen closets, a wonderful combination is dried lemon peel and dried lavender.

lemon and green olive salad

Olives and lemons—both are fruits, both sharply and vividly evoke aquamarine sea and that rough scrub of land called the Mediterranean.

Little chunks of peeled lemon and slivers of green olive combine in a tangy and refreshing "fruit salad" that begs to be scooped up in a piece of torn flatbread or spooned onto a thick slice of crusty country bread.

1 cup small green olives in brine, drained	1 tablespoon extra-virgin olive oil
2 lemons, preferably sweet Meyer lemons	$1/2$ teaspoon ground cumin
4 tablespoons chopped flat-leaf parsley	Fine sea salt and freshly ground black pepper
	SERVES 4

Pit olives and cut in half lengthwise. Or use a paring knife to slice olive flesh off pit in thick strips.

With a vegetable peeler, remove thin yellow skin from lemons. Leave white pith, or at least some of it. (The sweet and nutritious pith keeps the lemon segments intact.) Cut lemons into horizontal slices and pick out seeds. Following the pattern of the flesh, cut lemon slices into small segments.

Toss together olives and lemons, and season with remaining ingredients.

fresh potato chips

On a family trip to Sicily, I remember my then-small cousin Patrizia crying out in a pleading, plaintive little voice, *"Patatine, patatine,"* as we strolled through Villa Giulia, a park in Palermo where vendors sell roasted seeds, gelati, and other snacks. It was potato chips she wanted so desperately. And it was potato chips that she got.

Commercial potato chips are ubiquitous the world over. But the kind that line market shelves cannot compare with these freshly made, shatteringly crisp golden wafers.

A glass of cold white wine or Champagne goes well with them.

2 large baking potatoes, peeled
Fresh olive oil for frying
Fine sea salt

SERVES 4 (IF THEY SHOW A LITTLE RESTRAINT)

Slice potatoes into paper-thin wafers using a manual slicer or a knife. Soak in several changes of cold water until water runs clear. Drain wafers. Dry extremely well between tea towels to avoid splattering hot oil.

In a large, heavy saucepan, add enough olive oil to measure $1\frac{1}{2}$ inches in depth. Heat oil slowly until a piece of potato bubbles on contact and turns golden in about 2 minutes.

Cook potatoes in 2 or 3 batches, stirring constantly to prevent the chips from sticking to each other. Watch carefully and when golden, scoop out chips with a large Chinese wooden-handled strainer. Golden turns to dark brown in a second, so be careful not to overcook the chips. Drain on sheets of brown paper, and while still hot, sprinkle with salt.

sophisticated little pizza party

Champagne
Fresh Potato Chips
Pizza with Stracchino and Arugula
Espresso
Fruits in Kirschwasser

45.

frisella and tomato

If you thought biscotti were hard, wait until you bite into a frisella. Similar to hardtack, friselle, about the size of a bagel but without the hole, are baked just like biscotti, not once, but twice, until bone-dry. Without moisture, the bread has amazing keeping properties. I like to keep friselle on hand for those rare times when I run out of bread—an official state of emergency!

Friselle come from Apulia, located in the heel of the fancy high-heeled boot that is mainland Italy, and are made from durum or barley flour. After dipping the friselle in cool water, Apulians rub the surface with little tomatoes until the fruit breaks down into a coarse, shocking-red puree, and the juices seep into the bread.

Look for friselle in Italian markets. Or ask for gallette, the Ligurian equivalent. If neither is available a slice of dried country bread works fine (see Note).

2 friselle halves	2–3 arugula leaves
Spring water	Extra-virgin olive oil
1 garlic clove, peeled and cut in half crosswise	Fine sea salt and freshly ground black pepper
1 red, ripe tomato	Dried Mediterranean oregano
A few capers preserved in salt, soaked in cool water to remove excess saltiness	**MAKES 2**

Dip friselle halves into cool spring water. Lift out and with your hand, wipe away excess moisture.

Rub split sides with garlic. Cut tomato in half crosswise. Rub each frisella with a tomato half until the tomato breaks down into a coarse puree. Sprinkle with capers. Tear arugula into small fragments and scatter over top.

Drizzle with olive oil, and season with salt and pepper. Crumble oregano leaves over the top.

Note: If using dried country bread, there is no need to dip it in water first. Frisella has a fine, dense crumb that must be moistened first to bring it back to life. A loaf of country bread has many air pockets that soak up tomato juices quickly.

crisp bread squares with hot red pepper

You will become addicted to these crisp, fiery bread cubes—earthy and soulful, best washed down with a tumbler of fresh red wine poured from a pitcher.

When cubing the bread, consider the measurements a suggestion. Just don't make them too big or too small! A little variation in their size only adds to the rough charm of the dish.

Serve in a basket lined with either a coarse white cloth napkin or a piece of brown paper.

2 tablespoons extra-virgin olive oil	Fine sea salt
2 garlic cloves, peeled and lightly crushed	Dried Mediterranean oregano
1 sliver fresh hot red pepper or pinch hot red pepper flakes	
2 big, thick slices sturdy country bread, cut into 3/4-inch dice, about 2 cups diced bread	**SERVES 2 TO 3**

In a medium sauté pan, warm together olive oil, garlic, and hot red pepper. Add bread cubes, raise heat to medium, and toss until bread is golden and crisp on the outside but still somewhat soft within, a matter of a few minutes.

Off the heat, season with salt and oregano. Toss for a moment, then serve, either warm or at room temperature, in a basket lined with a clean white cloth or brown paper.

how fresh are your fresh herbs?

Although fresh herbs are becoming widely available these days, the quality often falls far from the mark. Really fresh herbs have a bounce to them, a buoyancy, a sign that they are full of life and juices.

Herbs at the mercy of supermarket rainstorms lose so much; the perfume in the oils vanishes into the air, the dampness changes the odors from sweet to foul, and they droop their sad heads.

Herbs cruelly jammed into too small plastic bags become bruised, which breaks down the structure of the leaves, changing their properties dramatically. Although this is especially true of tender basil, all herbs are affected negatively by careless treatment.

tender raw offerings

cleaning herbs

Please don't wash herbs under a hard stream of water. Herbs are delicate and bruise easily, and their perfumes become lost to the running water.

Imagine instead, a light, misty rain cleansing the herbs rather than a hard-driving rain that would surely damage them.

Dip herb leaves or sprigs in a bowl of cool water or rinse them under a gentle trickle of cool water from the faucet. Gently shake off the excess moisture and air-dry on tea towels.

persian spring herbs

A basket of fresh, tender herb sprigs is unparalleled perfection as a way to begin a meal—it has a living, breathing quality and a beautiful nakedness.

I always find refreshment nibbling on fresh herbs, feel excitement at the perfumes, the clean and vibrant flavors, the delicate forms the leaves take, and the many-shaded greens.

In springtime the custom in the Middle East is to collect wild herbs for this offering, the herbs symbolizing the first stirrings of life as the earth awakens from its long winter slumber. Wild sorrel is easy to find—in spring it virtually covers the ground in a soft green blanket; its lemony, grassy flavor is a milder version of sorrel; try to include it whenever possible.

Eat the herbs leaf by leaf, or wrap a tender sprig or two in a piece of torn flatbread. You can also serve tangy fresh white cheese made from sheep's milk, cut into cubes.

Choose some or all of the following.

Mint sprigs	Tarragon sprigs
Coriander sprigs	Wild sorrel sprigs
Dill sprigs	
Watercress sprigs	
Basil sprigs	
Small sorrel leaves	**SERVES AS FEW OR AS MANY AS YOU LIKE**

Gently wash herbs by dipping sprigs into a bowl of cool water. Gently shake off excess and dry on tea towels. Arrange the herbs in a basket and serve with flatbread.

american relish tray

It's a shame the classic American relish tray has fallen into disrepute. It's the fault of indifferent preparation, not any intrinsic problem with the offering itself. I'm sure the basic idea was influenced by European eating traditions, such as pinzimonio and crudités.

I've always been intrigued by this offering while being appalled by its slapdash execution: carrots that are all core, spongy celery with tough strings, canned olives.

But can you imagine how it must have looked and tasted at a fancy restaurant in the early part of the century: tender stalks of delicate celery, sugar-sweet carrots, some expertly cured "foreign" olives or crunchy brined cucumbers, sweet butter, and a finely crafted bread roll. All beautiful, refreshing, and serving their function of priming the appetite for the fancy courses that followed.

1 head crisp celery	Natural cucumber pickles (no preservatives or dyes)
1 bunch small to medium carrots	
1 bunch slender green onions	Unsalted butter
Black and green olives	Highest-quality bread rolls

Break off the outer tough stalks of celery until you arrive at the inner white stalks. Reserve outer stalks for another use. Detach pale celery stalks. If they are small, leave them whole; cut larger stalks in half crosswise.

Peel carrots. Cut into strips lengthwise. Trim root ends of green onions. Cut away any portion of green tops that looks yellowed or damaged, but leave fresh greenery intact.

Arrange prepared vegetables, olives, and pickles in serving dishes. Serve with sweet butter and rolls.

don't throw it away.

Very tender young radish leaves are delicious raw in salads; cut into strips and cooked, they are excellent with scrambled eggs. That's what Italians do with leftover radish greens from pinzimonio.

It was my first trip to Paris and I was

traveling with my mother and sisters. Our first evening, rather late, around eleven o'clock, my mother and I walked from our hotel to a nearby café. There we ate radishes and sweet butter and narrow, brittle-crusted baguettes, between sips of white wine of the house.

Outside, a light rain made the dark streets shine, and bands of gold from streetlights stretched across sidewalks and shop windows. As we walked back, people strolled by, faces obscured by umbrellas, talking and laughing, and the bitter-sweet smell of tobacco drifted into the cool night air.

eating radishes and butter in a Parisian café.

51.

fresh radishes and sweet butter

To do justice to this exquisitely simple offering, I suggest the following.

Find a source for or grow your own French Breakfast radishes, the variety the French serve with butter. Long and narrow in shape, two-toned dark pink and white, they have a mild peppery bite and are crisp, juicy, firm, and absolutely delicious. Or carefully select a bunch of small, firm radishes with bright green leafy tops. Big, old, overgrown radishes with spongy split flesh simply won't do!

Unsalted, or sweet, French or European-style butter is less watery and has a very light-on-the-tongue, rich dairy flavor. French-style butters made in America are available in many good markets. Or purchase a pure, preferably organic, unsalted butter.

It's the contrast of sweet butter, fine-crusted baguette, and crisp, tangy radish that makes this dish so appealing.

1 bunch small, firm radishes with fresh green leaves, preferably French Breakfast radishes

Unsalted butter

Fine sea salt

High-quality baguette, sliced just before serving

SERVES 4

Wash radishes well and remove all but a few of the smallest, nicest-looking leaves. Trim away long root ends. Dry radishes briefly on a tea towel.

Arrange radishes and bread in baskets. Offer butter in a thick slab and pass a small dish of salt for dipping radishes.

a cocktail and two Carpaccios

tomato cocktail, 1930

This is a version of tomato cocktail as served in America in the 1930s. Spoon it into small stemmed dishes and serve cool for a tangy starter to a summer meal.

5 very ripe summer tomatoes

½ teaspoon or more freshly grated horseradish

1 tablespoon very finely diced onion, lightly crushed

Lemon juice to taste

Fine sea salt and freshly ground black pepper

Lemon wedges

MAKES 4 SMALL SERVINGS

Peel, seed, and finely chop tomatoes. Drain well. Stir in horseradish, onion, and lemon juice. Refrigerate until cool.

Just before serving, season with salt and pepper. Spoon into small, shallow stemmed ice cream goblets or cocktail glasses. Garnish with lemon wedges. Serve immediately.

zucchini carpaccio with almonds

You've heard of raw beef carpaccio. Well, this is a raw vegetable carpaccio. The wafer-thin slices of raw young zucchini, topped with shavings of Parmesan, and almonds—look pale and exquisite and have a delicate and unusual flavor.

Young zucchini has a taste and texture that in no way resembles those of mature zucchini. Its sweetness and delicacy must be tasted raw to be fully appreciated. Select very fresh, firm small zucchini that are no longer than 5 to 6 inches, and no wider than 1 inch.

To make paper-thin slices of zucchini, purchase an inexpensive manual Japanese slicer, a more deluxe French mandoline, or simply use a very sharp knife. A vegetable peeler is the tool of choice for making Parmesan shavings.

1 dozen raw, unpeeled almonds	A few drops fresh lemon juice
1/4 pound fresh, young zucchini	Black pepper
Fine sea salt	
Piece of Parmesan cheese	
Extra-virgin olive oil	**SERVES 4**

Immerse the almonds in boiling water for 1 minute. Drain, then pop off the skins. Dry on a tea towel. Finely chop the almonds.

Working low over a large serving platter, carefully slice the zucchini and let fall on the platter, moving the slicer as you go in order to cover the platter evenly with a few thin layers. Salt the layers lightly.

Use a vegetable peeler to shave thin slices of cheese over the zucchini. Scatter the almonds over the top. Moisten with a little olive oil, a few drops of lemon juice, and a light grinding of black pepper. Serve no later than 15 minutes or so after preparing, as salt causes zucchini to shed water.

nature's juices

Tenderness and flavor lie in the juices of fresh fruits and vegetables, and those juices begin to leach out the minute the produce is harvested.

True freshness is fleeting; there is a world of difference between a freshly picked artichoke and one that is several days old. A fresh artichoke's fibers are swollen with juices so that a knife cuts through it easily, and the flavor is true and strong. Several days later, the taste becomes muted, like the faded colors of old cloth, and the flesh toughens.

vegetable carpaccio II

This recipe is a slightly more complex version of the vegetable carpaccio in my book *Verdura*. Here, the flavors are deepened by a touch of mustard and a scattering of capers, making it closer in spirit to the famous beef carpaccio that inspired it.

Why go to all the bother of slicing the vegetables so thinly? The paper-thin slicing serves many functions: It tenderizes dense vegetables such as artichokes and carrots; allows the juices locked in the fibers to come to the surface of each slice; and provides greater absorption of the dressing into the porous slices.

Aside from all this, the nearly transparent slices of vegetables look quite beautiful and delicate.

The following vegetables take very well to paper-thin slicing. Any one of them, save perhaps the leek (a bit too pungent), would be delicious served on its own in this way.

Small handful firm radishes, trimmed

1 each carrot, celery stalk from the heart, and leek

1 small fennel bulb

3 tablespoons extra-virgin olive oil

3 tablespoons lemon juice

1 teaspoon imported white wine mustard

Fine sea salt

1 heaping tablespoon small capers

1/2 lemon

1 medium artichoke

Small chunk of Parmesan cheese, enough to cover the vegetables with a layer of shavings, about 1 ounce

Black pepper

SERVES 4

Trim and very thinly slice all vegetables, except artichoke, using a manual slicer from France or Japan, or a trusty sharp knife.

In a bowl, combine olive oil, the 3 tablespoons of lemon juice, and mustard. Beat lightly with a fork. Season with salt. Stir in capers.

Use lemon half to rub cut portions of artichoke to prevent discoloration. Trim artichoke down to the heart. Thinly slice in same manner as other vegetables and immediately add to bowl. Quickly toss with dressing, to deter the darkening of the artichoke. Add remaining vegetables and toss gently.

Spread vegetables on a serving platter no more than two or three layers deep. Working over platter, use a vegetable peeler to lightly cover vegetables with shavings of Parmesan. Sprinkle with finely ground fresh pepper. If you wish, you can make the dish look a little glossy with drops of olive oil.

avocado spread

Avocados have been a part of my life since childhood, when I would be given them, by the boxful, from groves surrounding my best friend's house. And I always knew just the way I liked them best—coarsely mashed with salt and lemon juice, sometimes with a sprinkling of finely chopped green onions, spread on thin slices of lightly toasted Italian bread.

Avocado groves, once an important part of the Covina landscape, have vanished. But it only takes one taste of this beautiful green spread and I'm a child again, staring up through the dense leaves at the avocados dangling so temptingly from the tree branches.

A ripe but firm avocado has the truest flavor. Any brown areas of flesh, caused by bruising or overripening, must be scrupulously cut away. The dead, flat flavor of browned avocado destroys the astonishingly fresh taste of this unique fruit.

1 large Hass avocado, about 8 ounces, ripe but firm, at room temperature

3 tablespoons freshly squeezed lemon juice

¼ teaspoon fine sea salt

SERVES 2 TO 4

Use a mortar and pestle or a bowl and fork. Peel the avocado and place in the mortar or bowl. Add the lemon juice and salt, and coarsely mash the avocado until the lemon is blended in.

This is best served right away, but it holds up for about 30 minutes. Do not refrigerate. Serve with thin, warm, toasted rounds of Italian bread.

perfumed tomato dip

This deep red tomato dip is fragrant with lavish green coriander (cilantro) and garlic. Make it during the late summer months when tomatoes are truly ripe.

It makes a terrific party dip; everyone is intrigued by the dip's perfume and spice, and at least three people will ask you for the recipe, since very few will be able to pinpoint the origin of the enigmatic herbal flavor.

That it is so easy to make only contributes to its goodness. Make a big batch and serve with flatbreads.

4–5 tablespoons extra-virgin olive oil	6 sun-ripened tomatoes, peeled, chopped, and well drained in a colander
6 garlic cloves, peeled and finely chopped or crushed	Fine sea salt
1/4 teaspoon hot red pepper flakes or to taste	
1 big bunch fresh coriander (cilantro), leaves and tender stems chopped	**SERVES 6**

Warm olive oil, garlic, and hot red pepper flakes in a large sauté pan. Add coriander and stir for several minutes. Add the tomatoes and season with salt. Cook, uncovered, stirring often, over medium heat about 10 minutes, or until tomatoes turn into a thick sauce and thin juices evaporate. Quick cooking keeps the tomato flavor fresh.

Let cool.

Can be made up to a day in advance and returned to room temperature before serving. The perfume will be a bit muted but the dip will still taste very good.

farmer's cheese with chives

Farmer's cheese is a white, unripened cow's milk cheese with a fresh flavor and moist texture. Subtle and delicious, it is best accented by a generous handful of chives.

Chives demand to be in pristine condition, just picked fresh from the garden. I don't think I understood what chives were all about until I grew them myself. It is that elusive sweet-green onion perfume that makes chives so special. Now I use only the tender, willowy shoots that I harvest outside my kitchen door.

If you don't grow chives (and they are very easy to grow), chervil would be a lovely substitute along with a little finely chopped tarragon and flat-leaf parsley. Lemon thyme, chopped fine, would also be a good alternative.

1 pound farmer's cheese	Black pepper
¼ cup snipped fresh chives	
A little milk or extra-virgin olive oil	
Fine sea salt	**MAKES 1 POUND**

Use a fork to mash all ingredients together. Use about 5 tablespoons milk or 3 tablespoons olive oil, or enough of either to make the cheese a little creamy, and salt to taste. Mold cheese on a platter. Serve topped with coarsely ground black pepper.

You can also make the cheese up to an hour in advance, refrigerate, then return to cool room temperature. Just before serving, sprinkle with ground pepper.

fresh cheeses

entertaining

Don't be afraid to offer simple food to your guests. Elaborate pictures of fancy foods should remain on magazine pages. Simple food always elicits the strongest reactions—of thanks, of pleasure.

Let the message to your guests be: I honor you by taking the time to gather the best and freshest foods I can find, and I serve them to you in the spirit of sharing.

goat cheese and black olive cake

You're probably thinking, Oh no, not another layered cheese torta! The elaborate, many-layered tortas created of mascarpone and butter, striped with pesto or smoked salmon or dried figs, and made famous by Peck's in Milano, are quite extraordinary.

But this simple cake, or torta, is every bit as special, quite a bit leaner, and takes just a moment to make; it can be served an hour later. The 2 layers of chalk-white goat cheese surrounding 1 layer of gorgeous black-olive pesto looks a bit confectionary, like a white cake filled with dark chocolate.

Serve the cake with drinks before dinner. Or slice it thinly and accompany with a tender, lemony green salad for lunch.

10 ounces fresh goat cheese

2 teaspoons extra-virgin olive oil

Cheesecloth

3 tablespoons black-olive pesto, homemade or store-bought, flavored with a little finely chopped lemon zest

SERVES 4

Combine goat cheese and olive oil, and mash with a fork until creamy and smooth.

Moisten cheesecloth and squeeze out any excess water. Line a small container with a double thickness of cheesecloth, letting excess hang over sides. Pack with half the goat cheese. Pat it down with your fingers until evenly distributed. Spoon black-olive pesto over goat cheese and spread it evenly over cheese. Top with other half of goat cheese. Pat down until evenly spread. Cover with overhanging cheesecloth.

Refrigerate, with a can or other weight on the cheese to compress layers, for at least 1 hour and up to 1 to 2 days.

To unmold, carefully peel away cheesecloth covering top of cheese. Upend on serving platter, gently tug at cheesecloth to free it from cheese, then carefully peel off.

Serve surrounded with crostini, or cut into thin slices or wedges to accompany a green salad.

labneh with crushed mint

This fresh cheese begins with goat's milk yogurt. When drained of liquid, the yogurt becomes transformed into a tart, creamy, and lean spread.

Fragrantly herbal from a scattering of pungent dried mint, the cheese is enriched with a little puddle of glossy olive oil that merges with the cheese as you dip in your flatbread.

Goat's milk yogurt is available in natural food stores. If the sharp, lemony tang doesn't please you, substitute cow's milk yogurt for a sweeter taste.

Cheesecloth, folded in 4 layers, enough to line a colander	Crushed dried mint
1 quart goat's milk yogurt	Extra-virgin olive oil
Fine sea salt	**MAKES 1 PINT**

Line a colander with damp, folded cheesecloth. Place the colander in a large bowl. Add a little salt to the yogurt in the container and stir. Upend the container and let the yogurt fall into the cloth.

Drain all day or overnight, or until the yogurt is dense and creamy. Scrape the cheese from the cheesecloth into a bowl. Taste and add salt as needed. Refrigerate.

To serve, spoon the labneh into a rustic bowl. With the back of a spoon, make a shallow depression in the middle. Sprinkle the cheese with mint, crushing the dried leaves between your fingers to release the scent. Pool a little olive oil in the center. Serve with flatbread.

ricotta fresca

Most storebought versions of ricotta—with grainy texture, dense and heavy on the tongue—are diametrically opposite to the billowy fresh texture and sweet taste of true ricotta. Of commercially available ricotta, whole milk ricotta comes closest to the qualities I associate with fine ricotta.

Artisanal ricotta, made by small companies, is often of superior quality.

When you've found a source for high-quality ricotta, try a little of it, slightly warmed, on a crust of bread. Top it with a thread of olive oil, crushed black pepper, and sea salt, and let the perfumes rise to your nose.

breakfast, brunch, and

Beyond

65.

breakfast will never be the same again

Rice pudding? Sandwiches? Coffee granita? What are these dishes doing in the breakfast chapter?

You'll be disappointed if you look for waffles in this chapter. And what you do find may confound your notions of what breakfast should be. In challenging our accepted notions of what breakfast is all about, the following recipes might be considered downright radical.

I didn't grow up in a pancakes-and-sausages house. My mornings most often began with hot milk flavored with a few drops of coffee and slices of buttered bread. After all, that is the traditional Italian breakfast.

As my Italian mother began to accustom herself to the ways of her new culture, she would occasionally make pancakes (she loves them!) or prepare thin delicate frittatas for breakfast (instead of supper, which is when Italians eat frittatas).

Perhaps it was my aversion to runny eggs—poached, soft-boiled, or fried—that prevented me from joining the ranks. But when it comes to breakfast, I go my own way.

At first you may balk at disrupting sacred morning rituals by introducing new foods that don't conform to what we consider a socially acceptable breakfast. So I suggest that you ease into some of the more unusual (to us) morning foods. Saturday and Sunday brunch might be the right time to begin, since it is the first meal of the day and often less-than-typical dishes are served. Brunch's late-morning starting time allows us to partake in a wide variety of different eating experiences.

It was in *Verdura* that I offered my first breakfast recipe, an Italian summer breakfast (I sneaked it into the dessert chapter) of lemon granita and brioche.

Then came *panini, bruschetta, crostini,* where I suggest serving certain panini and bruschetta for breakfast—a sweetly fragrant lemon frittata panino; grilled bread with a topping of ricotta and fresh fruit, among others.

This, my first official breakfast chapter ever, dips generously into foods we want to eat today—fresh vegetables, wholesome breads, fruits (fresh and dried), grains, beans, and lean cheeses—and introduces them into the morning mix.

Some of the dishes simply bring together good ingredients, such as yogurt and rose preserves; others are the work of a moment (Tender Egg Island Style, see page 80). All the breakfasts are healthy and vigorous; some will surprise you when you learn how truly fortifying they are.

It has been drummed into our heads that breakfast is the most important meal of the day. With the rushed pace of life today, it is often the only true nutrition we provide our bodies until dinner.

If you're willing to depart from tradition—for reasons of health, to bring more of the beauty and flavors of the garden to the breakfast table, or for a great adventure—forget about fried eggs or cold cereal one morning and try something new.

Breakfast will never be the same again!

We were at our breakfast under a tree in the garden. Madame Dupart had brought us a basket of cherries, rolls, and a pot of steaming coffee. Through the foliage, arrows of early sunlight broke upon our table, and one quivered in the goblet of chill yellow wine that Denis raised to admire its brilliance. His sigh reflected our feelings. Why on such a perfect day as this should our felicity be broken by the wrench of departure?

Chef's holiday, Idwal Jones, 1952 (IDWAL)

breakfast in italy

Rolls, such as a rosetta or michetta, or a cornetto (croissant), or a brioscia (brioche), and a foamy cappuccino or caffè latte are the components of a classic Italian breakfast, *la prima colazione*.

Whether breakfast is taken at home or enjoyed at the corner café, the only accompaniments might be a little sweet butter (the only time Italians use butter on bread) or a bit of jam.

Although it may strike one as an altogether frivolous way to begin the day, remember that good bread has protein, and so does milk. And if you decide to start the day Italian style, keep with Italian tradition: Make lunch the most substantial meal of the day, and at the end of the day have a light *cena*, evening supper.

Italian-style sweet (not sourdough) roll	Jam, optional
Unsalted butter	Caffè latte

Tear or cut open roll and spread lightly with butter. Spread with jam or not, as desired. Serve with steaming-hot caffè latte.

Sweet butter is butter made without the addition of salt. The taste of unsalted butter can be a shock to those who only know the salted variety.

On my first family trip to Italy, at age twelve, I remember tasting unsalted butter for the first time. I was sitting on the balcony of our hotel in Taormina, perched atop a dry, craggy hillside covered with wild prickly-pear cactus and blossoming oleander that sloped gently to the sparkling aquamarine sea. It was the same hotel where my parents had spent their *luna di miele*, their honeymoon.

I thought the butter had a strangely flat quality, because I was used to the overpowering taste of salt in butter. The flavor was different from what I was used to, but sweet, creamy, and oddly delicious spread on my morning roll.

Salt acts as a preservative; but its flavor can also cover up traces of rancidity. With saltless butter, there is nowhere to hide, so it must be scrupulously fresh. European butter also tends to be richer than our butter; a little goes a long way.

Now, it is salted butter that tastes strange to me—the saltiness almost obliterating the subtly sweet cream flavor. And I always use sweet butter on my bread and in all my cooking.

A very important storage note: Keep unsalted butter in the freezer to maintain freshness.

Tasting butter in TAORMINA.

jams and marmalades I like

Bread and butter spread with jam may seem pedestrian and prosaic, but when the bread is a hearth-baked rustic loaf, when the butter is sweet, and when the jam is homemade or crafted by good jam makers, it becomes a sublime treat.

Where to look for good jams? Try farmer's markets, ethnic markets, or stores that stock specialty foods. Most supermarkets carry quite an extensive selection. Also see Lemon Carrot Marmalade (page 286), Spanish Tomato Marmalade (page 287), and others in the chapter on preserves that you can easily make at home. In these recipes, no canning is required—just refrigerate the jam and use within a month or so.

When purchasing jams, make sure to read the label carefully. Look for products that are free of chemicals and other unwanted additives. Let the pure fruit flavor be the guiding star in your search.

Sampling new jams adds a touch of adventure to the breakfast table, so be daring and try something totally different.

The following are some of my favorites. I provide producers' names where I think the information might be useful.

Ginger preserves, Jaime Keiller & Sons, Manchester, England
Quince jam, Cortas, Beirut, Lebanon
Fig jam (with roasted sesame seeds and musk), Agrosyr, Damascus, Syria
Grapefruit marmalade
Bitter orange marmalade, made from Seville oranges
Rose preserves (without artificial color if possible)

children's bread and milk soup

In Sicily children often eat this "soup" of hot milk, bread, and a few drops of coffee for breakfast. It is similar to the French custom of dipping bread into *café au lait*. The use of Sicily's own bread—made from hard-wheat golden durum flour and sesame seeds—is what makes it so special. And nutritious, since both flour and sesame seeds contain protein.

Sicilian bread has a sturdy crumb, a crisp, substantial crust, and a special flavor. But you can also use other wholesome, full-bodied rustic breads.

If this breakfast sounds appealing, and you're all grown up, just add more espresso to the "soup." That's what I do!

Milk	1 slice day-old Sicilian Bread (see page 296)
Freshly brewed espresso	
Sugar	**SERVES 1**

Pour hot milk into a European-style extra-large cup or small sturdy bowl. Add a few drops of espresso. Stir in sugar to taste. Cut several small squares of bread, and add to hot milk. Wait a moment until the bread absorbs some of the milk and softens. Then eat with a big spoon.

breakfast granita

Everyone loves coffee granita. Those dark brown, glittering grains of ice have an instant cooling effect on the mind and body.

In America granita has become a dessert. But Italians enjoy granita as an afternoon refresher, to be slowly spooned into one's mouth on a sultry summer day. Coffee granita is also a way to begin that same torrid day when you need something cold and revivifying.

Top it with a dollop of *unsweetened* whipped cream, to take the edge off, but not obscure, the coffee's strong flavor. And serve with a nice brioscia—brioche in Italian.

2 cups hot, freshly made espresso or dark-roasted coffee	Unsweetened whipped cream
¼ cup sugar	**MAKES 4 SERVINGS**

Stir together espresso and sugar until sugar dissolves.

Pour sweetened espresso into a metal pie dish and place in freezer. Remove from freezer and stir about every 20 minutes. Scrape down sides of dish, break up ice, and stir into granita. Continue until all liquid has turned to slushy ice crystals.

It is now ready to eat. Or transfer to a glass or plastic container with a secure lid, and place back in freezer; it will keep for a few weeks.

tasting yogurt and perfume

As I sat eating my yogurt topped with rose preserves, I felt like a voluptuary. The scent of roses captured in a sugary essence had the impact of perfume, only it was a perfume that one could taste.

Was I in Morocco sitting on a carpet in a walled garden, listening to the cooling sound of water from a small fountain? No. I was eighteen, and on my own exploring San Francisco for the first time, when I stepped into that small Middle Eastern café.

Tart yogurt with a bit of flowery sweet jam in it has the same voluptuous power over me today as it did then.

Early morning visiting is usual as everyone gets up before dawn while the air is fresh and cool. A brisk walk to a friend's house gives one a chance to view a paradise of fruit trees. As the guest arrives, coffee and sun-ripened apricots, grapes, and honey-filled figs are placed on tables inlaid with mother-of-pearl. Early breakfast is the time for gossip—and sampling the dainty dishes. A few hours later, at home, regular breakfast consists of coffee, olives, zahter (thyme with sumac), scrambled eggs covered with Kamoun (powdered cuminseed), kareeshee (cheese), and bread, which is considered the "staff of life" in the entire Middle East. (*The Art of Syrian Cooking*, Helen Corey, 1962)

rice pudding cake

A pudding that is simply rice and milk cooked with a touch of sugar. It is wonderfully refreshing served cool on a hot summer morning. And the pure white rice with its dark dusting of cinnamon looks fresh and inviting.

For a rose-scented pudding, replace the cinnamon with a few drops of rose water, stirred into the rice in the final moments of cooking.

$^1/_2$ cup Arborio or other short-grain rice

$1^1/_2$ cups spring water

1 quart milk

Pinch fine sea salt

2 tablespoons sugar or to taste

Ground cinnamon

MAKES 4 SMALL SERVINGS

Bring rice and water to a boil. Simmer for 15 minutes. Add milk, salt, and sugar. Bring to a boil, then simmer for 30 minutes, or until the pudding is lightly thick and creamy. Stir occasionally during first 20 minutes of cooking, more frequently during last 10 minutes. Remember, the pudding will firm up as it chills.

Spoon into serving dishes and chill. Serve with a generous dusting of cinnamon.

breakfast from the garden

When the garden or the market is in full seasonal swing, why not bring some of the bounty into the morning kitchen? Fruits and vegetables are as delicious eaten early in the morning as at other times of the day. The following are just a few ideas culled from other chapters in this book.

On a spring morning, try fresh-tasting, herbal Spinaci Villa Amore (see page 226), enriched with a scattering of Parmesan cheese. A good way to start the day.

In summer Tomato in Nature (see page 88), a salad of juicy tomatoes and fragrant mint, is easily assembled and refreshing. Just right on a hot summer morning served with a slice of country bread.

A dish of garlicky Roasted Sweet and Hot Peppers (see page 220) left over from the night before tastes wonderful first thing on a hot, lazy morning in early fall. Not scrambled into eggs or used as a bed for a poached egg (although both would be good, too), but simply served with bread for soaking up the syrupy sweet-hot juices.

Cherries and Almonds (see page 306) are sublime served on a lovely June morning.

A soft spring day seems to call for a basket of strawberries and Rice Pudding Cake (see page 74).

In winter a fruit macedonia (see page 324) of kiwi, bananas (red ones would be nice), and oranges is simple to make and full of goodness.

The morning was full of golden sunlight.

We had coffee in a rustic arbor in the garden: also dark honey three summers old, and butter of the day, which we spread on croissants hot from the brick oven. Also we had little blocks of cheese, the *Fromage de Curé* of the parish, supposed to be made only for prelates, and the taste of it is memorable to this day.

Jeannot, who knew not sleep, waited upon us. The coffee was fiercely hot, and the garden was full of the scent of its roasting, also with the scents of ivy, the tall delphiniums, and the foliage of the ripening tomatoes.

Chef's holiday, Idwal Jones, 1952
(IDWAL)

sandwiches and bruschetta for breakfast

Bruschetta or a sandwich for breakfast? Yes, indeed. When made with whole-some bread and fresh fruits, lean cheeses and nuts, a sandwich or bruschetta can be a nourishing and delicious way to start the day. They take a moment to prepare and they are portable—on those unfortunate mornings when we must rush out the door.

Here are a few suggestions for what to make first thing in the morning.

Sandwiches

Panino di Papà (see page 140) with fresh ricotta and walnuts on whole-grain bread

Peach Sandwich (see page 148), slices of ripe peaches between buttered and sugared bread

Tomato and Oregano Panino (see page 141), a sandwich of juicy, cool tomato slices—refreshing on a hot summer morning

Bruschetta

Grilled bread with sun-warmed grapes (see page 152)—as easy as toasting a thick slice of bread, rubbing it with garlic and grabbing a bunch of grapes

Grilled Bread with Goat Cheese and Honey (see page 153), warmed or not—delicious on toasted bread for breakfast

fresh eggs

Eggs can be judged in the same way we assess the ripeness of a peach or the freshness of a mushroom. Although we can't see inside the shell, it is still possible to determine an egg's worth.

Chickens that roam around and scratch the earth in the way nature intended produce eggs of higher quality. Chickens fed the right grains and allowed to search for their own natural foods (grasses, tiny worms, insects) produce eggs of higher nutritive value and better flavor. Also remember that the addition of hormones and antibiotics to the diets of chickens certainly does not benefit the consumer (the animal's diet becomes part of your diet).

A very fresh egg is of more nutritional value than one many days (or weeks) old. Since the white of an egg turns liquidy when the egg is old, cup the egg in its shell in your hand and move it gently, or hold it close to your ear and gently shake to detect any movement of the yolk in the liquid.

The freshest eggs also taste the best.

Once you crack open an egg, assessing its quality becomes easier. The yolk of a fresh egg is high and rounded, and the white clings to it in a thick mass. The color of the yolk will be a deep, vivid shade of orange. Smell it. Is the egg sweetly fragrant?

Avoid buying mass-produced commercial eggs. With their pale yolks and attenuated flavor, and their compromised nutritive value, they are just a shadow of the real thing.

A late morning breakfast on a small Italian Island.

Blood Orange Juice

Tender Egg Island Style

Ripe Figs

Caffè Latte

tender egg island style

Imagine you are on a small rocky island in the Mediterranean. The sea is aquamarine, translucent. You are sitting alone on the terrace of a small rustic house, shaded from the sun by a bamboo awning. It is morning but already fiercely hot. What to make for breakfast? A cooling little "salad" of tomato, egg, mint, and crostini.

1 small tomato, peeled and cut into small chunks

1 hard-cooked egg, preferably organic

4–5 small chunks lightly toasted country bread

Fine sea salt and coarsely ground black pepper

1 tablespoon finely diced Pecorino Romano cheese or other tangy hard cheese

4 mint leaves

1 teaspoon extra-virgin olive oil

SERVES 1

Scatter tomato chunks in center of plate. Cut egg in half and nestle into tomatoes. Surround egg with croutons. Season with salt and pepper. Sprinkle with cheese and tear mint leaves over the top. Drizzle with olive oil.

herbs—when to chop

Never chop fresh herbs in advance. They should be chopped at the last moment or they lose their vibrance.

eggs stuffed with herbs and nasturtiums

Green herbs and the young leaves and flowers of nasturtiums flavor these tender hard-cooked eggs—served for breakfast or brunch, or as a luncheon dish. The nasturtiums add a peppery quality that contrasts nicely with the sweet richness of the eggs. A thin slice off the base of each egg steadies it on the plate.

To take along on a picnic, reassemble the egg halves, wrap each in a big green leaf of butter lettuce, and secure with a toothpick. Serve with some cool white wine.

2 hard-cooked eggs, preferably organic

3–4 small nasturtium leaves and tender stems, chopped

2 nasturtium flowers, cut into fine strips

1 sprig each chervil and flat-leaf parsley, chopped

1 skinny green onion, white and pale green parts finely chopped

Extra-virgin olive oil

Fine sea salt and coarsely ground black pepper

MAKES 4

Cut eggs in half lengthwise and carefully remove yolks. Place yolks in a small bowl. Add nasturtiums, herbs, and green onion. Mash with a fork, adding enough olive oil, just a drizzle, to make a paste. Season with salt and pepper.

Lightly salt egg whites. Gently fill cavities with egg yolk and herb mixture. Grind a little pepper over the top.

edgewater beach hotel, 1926

Soft scrambled eggs are spooned into the hollows of fresh summer peaches, which are nestled into a bed of tender green leaves. This refreshing and lovely dish was served at the famous Edgewater Beach Hotel in Chicago. The eggs go well with chilled white wine, cold champagne, or iced tea scented with sweet herbs.

For an extra flourish, you can drape a few slivers of prosciutto over the eggs before serving.

2 large, ripe, fragrant peaches

1 tablespoon unsalted butter

2 eggs, preferably organic

1–2 tablespoons cream, optional but good

Fine sea salt and freshly ground black pepper

Tender sprigs of watercress or small, sweet lettuce leaves

Snipped chives

SERVES 2 TO 4

Dip peaches in boiling water for a few seconds. Let cool a bit, then peel. Cut peaches in half and remove pits. Cut a thin slice off each base to stabilize peach halves.

Melt butter in a small sauté pan. Beat eggs with a fork, and stir in cream, if desired. Season with salt and pepper. Add to sauté pan and scramble gently over low heat until large, soft curds form.

Arrange a few salad greens on plates. Place 2 peach halves in the center of each plate and spoon in scrambled eggs. Snip chives over eggs and grind black pepper on top.

This recipe can easily be increased to serve more people. The eggs can be served warm or at room temperature—but only just when they reach room temperature.

persian herb pie

In this savory pie, it is not just the customary tablespoon or two of herbs for flavor but big fragrant mounds. Think of the herbs as leafy greens, just as you do the sweet lettuce leaves that accompany them.

This is a dish that celebrates the advent of spring. Surround it with young leafy radishes and serve it forth, not just as morning food, but for lunch and dinner too.

1 cup each chopped flat-leaf parsley and coriander, leaves and tender stems only

1/2 cup snipped garden chives or finely chopped green onions

1/2 cup slivered sweet lettuce leaves (butterhead and other loose-leaf lettuces, and young tender romaine)

2 garlic cloves, peeled and finely chopped

6 eggs, preferably organic

Fine sea salt and black pepper

2 tablespoons extra-virgin olive oil

SERVES 4

In a large bowl, mix together herbs, lettuces, and garlic. In a medium bowl, lightly beat eggs, and season with salt and freshly ground pepper. Stir herb mixture into eggs.

Heat a small, seasoned oven-proof skillet. When hot, add olive oil and swirl to coat pan (see Note). Off heat, add egg mixture. Transfer pan to top shelf of a 350° oven and cook until top is set and pie filling is firm.

Remove from oven and cool for a minute or two. Slide or invert pie onto a serving plate. Serve barely warm or at room temperature, cut into squares or wedges.

Note: This dish can also be baked in a standard pie tin or square cake pan. Just swirl oil in hot pan, add mixture and proceed as directed.

Summer

Labneh with Crushed Mint (see page 63)
Wedges of Tomato
Slices of Mediterranean or English Cucumber
Oil-Cured Black Olives
Flatbread
Fresh Apricots and Almonds

, two middle eastern breakfasts .

Winter

Ful Mdammas with Squeezed Lime (see page 85)
Flatbread
Green Olives
Dried Fruits: Dates, Apricots, and Figs

ful mdammas with squeezed lime

Ful mdammas, a traditional breakfast dish of the eastern Mediterranean, is made of small, round, dark brown dried fava beans. While I've enjoyed ful prepared in various ways, this version is extraordinary and my favorite. It was given to me by the owner of a small Middle Eastern market where I shop. As he spoke, a faraway, dreamy expression came into his eyes, and a look of sadness, too. No doubt he was thinking of his homeland and lost way of life. His ful, perfumed with tart lime and the fire of crushed hot green peppers, is truly memorable.

It is everyday dishes such as this one that people remember and crave, for they represent home to those lost souls in exile, or those separated from their culture by the vagaries of life. Although the custom is to serve it for breakfast, ful is equally good served as the centerpiece of lunch or dinner.

2 cups cooked ful mdammas plus a little of the bean broth, or 1 15-ounce can ful with broth (see Note)

1 large garlic clove, peeled

1-inch piece thin hot green pepper, fresh or pickled

Fine sea salt

Juice of 1 to 2 limes

1 tablespoon extra-virgin olive oil

Lime wedges

SERVES 4

Gently warm beans, crushing them on the side of the pan using a wooden spoon. Add bean broth a little at a time until a thick, rough-textured loose puree forms.

With a mortar and pestle, grind garlic and hot green pepper with salt to form a creamy paste. Off heat, stir mixture into beans. Stir in olive oil. Squeeze limes over beans and stir. Taste for salt.

Place in a shallow bowl, with a puddle of olive oil in the middle of the puree. Garnish with thick lime wedges. Serve with flatbread.

Note: Canned ful mddamas is a convenient alternative to the long cooking time required for this dried bean. No amount of cooking seems to soften the tough skins. When buying canned beans, look for a brand made without additives. The beans should emerge from the can whole, tender, and creamy.

living salads

87.

tomato in nature

A sun-ripened, tart-sweet tomato, full of juice and luscious red flesh, still enveloped in the fragrance of its green leaves requires very little in the way of embellishment. Olive oil and red wine vinegar are the usual condiments.

But it occurred to me that a really good tomato doesn't require any dressing at all. So, I've "dressed" this salad with fragments of tangy cheese, fresh mint, and garlic—without even a drop of olive oil or vinegar!

1 beautiful ripe but firm tomato	A little finely diced garlic
Fine sea salt	2–3 mint leaves
1 tablespoon finely sliced and crumbled Pecorino Romano cheese	**SERVES 1**

Cut tomato into wedges and season with salt. Sprinkle with cheese and garlic. Tear mint leaves over salad. Eat right away.

salads in the raw.

tomatoes and the big chill

Don't refrigerate fresh tomatoes. Cold temperatures destroy their texture.

The cold also arrests any further ripening. Since supermarket tomatoes are sold woefully underripe, further ripening at home is absolutely necessary. Also, a cold tomato has less flavor than one at room temperature—the chill blocks the flavor and deadens the fragrance.

In salads a room-temperature tomato has a fuller flavor and spicier perfume. For example, when making Caprese, a tomato and mozzarella salad, warm the tomatoes a bit by placing them on a sunny ledge before slicing them.

the fig tree at home

In late summer the fig tree in my mother's yard is full of fruit. This tree was my father's pride—he would jealously stand guard over the figs, chasing away greedy, fig loving birds, waiting and watching for the moment the fruits were ripe.

fresh fig salad

Figs ripen all at once when, in late summer, the weather turns fiercely hot and the air is so still it's eerie. Overnight the unyielding green fruits turn into plump purple-black bundles dusted with pale blue bloom; inside, the flesh is rose-colored and honey-sweet.

Ripe figs beg to be eaten out of hand without embellishment. However, if you have an abundance of them, you can make this lovely salad. The purple skin of the figs turns the dressing of olive oil, citrus juices, and honey a rosy pink.

12 ripe Mission figs or any other variety of fig	$1/3$ cup raw walnut halves, very coarsely broken up
2 tablespoons extra-virgin olive oil	$1/3$ cup roughly chopped mint leaves
2 tablespoons lemon juice	Freshly ground black pepper
1 tablespoon orange juice	
1 teaspoon honey	**SERVES 4**

Cut figs in quarters and place on serving platter. Combine olive oil, lemon juice, orange juice, and honey in a small bowl, and beat lightly with a fork.

Sprinkle walnuts and mint over figs. Drizzle with dressing and toss very gently. Grind a little pepper over the top. Let rest for a few minutes before serving.

don't throw it away.

Do not remove the white pith when peeling oranges for savory salads or when eating out of hand. Contrary to popular belief, the pith is sweet and delicious, with a delightfully soft, cushiony texture. And it is good for you, too.

orange and leek salad

Oranges, olive oil, salt—three words that resonate for me in a special way. They make me think of my mother, who has always had a passion for orange salads.

To this trio, I've added rings of tender raw leek. The crisp, juicy rings are pungent without being too hot—an aromatic, exciting contrast to the glistening, sweet-liquid oranges.

1 medium leek, white and palest green portions only	Fine sea salt and black pepper
3 juicy oranges	
Extra-virgin olive oil	**SERVES 2 TO 4**

Slice trimmed leek into thin rings. Separate rings and rinse in cold water to remove any hidden grit. Drain and dry well.

Peel and cut oranges into slices or chunks. Arrange prepared oranges on a serving dish and scatter leeks over top. Drizzle salad with olive oil, and season with salt and freshly ground pepper. Toss gently.

tabbouleh party

Tabbouleh is more than a salad in a deli case. It is one of the great salads of the world, refreshing and nutritious. When eaten from a communal bowl, using small, tender grape leaves plucked from under a shady grape arbor for scoops, a true communion takes place. A friend of mine recalled with pleasure the ritual of a large platter of tabbouleh shared at mealtime on hot summer days in Lebanon. To accompany the salad, tall ice cube–filled glasses of water topped with that powerhouse Middle Eastern drink, anise-flavored arak.

Why not follow this custom and have a tabbouleh party, where everyone eats from the same serving bowl? Set the bowl under a grape arbor or shady tree or in a garden, and surround with young grape leaves, large basil leaves, or tender lettuce leaves.

There are only a few secrets to making great tabbouleh. First and foremost, parsley is the main ingredient—a mountain of parsley interspersed with a sprinkling of bulghur. And the parsley must be the flat-leaf variety, not curly parsley, which is too tough and fibrous. And it should be drenched in tart and aromatic —and here's a twist—lime juice, also a part of Middle Eastern cooking, which I use instead of lemons for its slightly resinous perfume.

¹/₂ cup bulghur	6 tablespoons extra-virgin olive oil
¹/₂ cup spring water	6 tablespoons freshly squeezed lime juice
Fine sea salt	1 large, ripe but firm tomato, finely diced
3 big bunches flat-leaf parsley, about 2 cups chopped	Ground sumac, a nonpoisonous berry with a unique lemony flavor, optional but nice (available in Middle Eastern markets)
2 bunches mint leaves, about ¹/₂ cup slivered	
¹/₂ cup finely diced spring onion or sliced green onions	Tender grape leaves, wild or cultivated, large basil leaves, or lettuce leaves
1 medium-sized Middle Eastern or English cucumber, peeled, seeded, and finely diced	**SERVES 2 TO 4**

In a small bowl, combine bulghur, water, and a little salt. Stir and set aside.

After washing, let parsley dry completely. Finely chop leaves and tender stems. Working with washed and well-dried mint, stem leaves and finely sliver.

In a large shallow bowl, combine parsley, mint, onion, and cucumber. With your palms, press out excess water from bulghur and sprinkle over top.

Drizzle with olive oil and lime juice, and toss, adding salt to taste. Scatter tomato over the top and sprinkle top with sumac. Serve with leaf of choice, or a selection.

persimmon, avocado, and grapefruit salad, 1920s

It may sound trendy, but versions of this salad appear in American cookbooks in the 1920s.

Serve this gorgeous salad as a first course for Thanksgiving. It's very festive-looking with bright, jewellike colors. The contrasting flavors get dinner off to a light and refreshing start.

Use equal amounts of persimmon and grapefruit and slightly less avocado. Ripe Fuyu persimmons are firm, crisp, and juicy. Hachiyas, which must be soft as jam to be fully ripe, do not work well.

2 Fuyu persimmons, peeled and sliced

2 pink grapefruit, peeled and cut into segments, all juices saved

Extra-virgin olive oil

Juice of ½ small orange

Fine sea salt

Avocado, firm yet ripe, peeled and cut into dice, tossed with a little lemon juice to prevent darkening

Coarsely chopped walnuts (black walnuts if available)

Watercress sprigs

SERVES 4

Place prepared persimmons and grapefruit in a shallow serving bowl. Drizzle with olive oil, orange juice, and reserved grapefruit juice, and season with salt. Toss gently. Scatter avocado and walnuts over the top. Garnish with watercress sprigs.

misery salad

In this elegant, cool-looking salad, a tart creamy dressing lightly cloaks half-moons of pale green cucumber.

The name of the salad refers to the water, or "tears," the cucumbers shed when salted.

1 English cucumber, peeled, cut in half lengthwise, and seeded	1 tablespoon chopped flat-leaf parsley leaves
Fine sea salt	1 finely diced shallot
½ cup crème fraîche or labneh, drained until the consistency of thick cream (see page 63)	Black pepper
3 teaspoons lemon juice	**SERVES 4**

Salt cucumber and drain cut side down on several layers of tea towels. Wipe dry after 30 minutes. Thinly slice cucumber and place in a bowl.

Add crème fraîche, lemon juice, parsley, and shallot. Stir gently until cucumber slices are lightly coated. Taste and add salt if necessary. Grind pepper over top. Salad can be made 1 hour before serving. Refrigerate until ready to serve.

ginger carrot salad

Grated carrots, marinated in orange juice, fresh ginger, and hot red pepper, create a spicy refreshing salad.

A variation of this salad appears in the thin volume of recipes accompanying a 1969 *Time-Life* book on Middle Eastern cooking that I unearthed while leafing through cookbooks in the dim recesses of the old San Francisco public library. In the book, they suggest spooning the carrots into avocado halves, a lovely idea, although the carrot salad is perfection in and of itself.

By the way, don't even think of discarding the juices that remain in the bowl after the carrots have had their bath. The juices make a sensational spicy-sweet drink.

$1/2$–$3/4$ pound carrots, about 2 cups grated	$1/8$ teaspoon peeled and finely chopped fresh ginger
1 cup freshly squeezed orange juice	Fine sea salt
$1/8$ teaspoon hot red pepper flakes	**SERVES 4**

Peel and grate carrots on the largest holes of a four-sided grater. Combine carrots, hot red pepper flakes, ginger, and salt to taste in a bowl. Cover and chill for at least 1 hour.

With a slotted spoon, lift out carrot mixture, letting excess carrot juices drain back into bowl. Serve.

leaves from nature, wild and cultivated

green leaves.

I feel a keen excitement when I sit down to eat a dish of beautiful green leaves. It satisfies me in a way no other food can. Eating tender lettuce leaves gives me a direct link to nature. In fact, some of the greens growing in a meadow after a spring rain can be used to compose delightful salads.

For example, in a large wilderness area near my home, early spring brought with it fields of miner's lettuce with delicate leaves, as green as spring itself, shaped like spades, each leaf centered with a tiny white blossom as small as the head of a pin. Dressed with a few drops of olive oil and lemon juice, the salad is the essence of spring.

Many wild greens have their cultivated counterpart. You can grow lamb's lettuce and purslane in your backyard. Arugula, a plant that grows wild in Italy, is also eaten as a cultivated plant. In America you can grow it from seed.

Watercress, too, grows wild in America, and as its name implies, it likes water to be nearby as it grows. Domestic watercress has been widely available for a long time—and I'm an ardent fan. Since watercress has always been around, it may elicit less excitement than more voguish leaves, but its extraordinary flavor and high nutritive value make it worth discovering anew.

Cultivated lettuces—romaine, butter, limestone, red oak—all add to the beauty and flavor of the salad bowl. And most markets sell young leaves of various lettuces and greens, both sweet and pungent, separately and in combination.

Always look for leaves with a springy quality, since this means the leaf fibers are bursting with juices. Search out deep green leaves or other rich, true colors—an indication of high vitamin and mineral content.

Newly introduced to supermarkets are organic salad greens, especially important since the leaf is eaten in its entirety, without the peeling and trimming other vegetables require that eliminate surface pesticides.

Salads of tender raw leaves sparkling with the simplest dressings are one of the most important components of healthy eating. Green is the color of immortality. Is it because greens keep the body young?

going to the source

Each day that elapses after a fruit or vegetable is picked, there is a loss in nutrition, a dulling of flavor, and a diminishment of natural juices. That is why it is so important to purchase your produce at its source, or as near to it as possible.

A just-picked lemon will have stronger, more deeply aromatic oils in the peel than one that was picked even only hours before. Harvesting lettuce leaves in the garden right before supper creates a romantic vision, but it also allows us to derive the full benefits from each ruffled, fragile leaf.

romaine for the ages

Romaine, one of the finest lettuces to find its way into the salad bowl, has been eaten and appreciated since antiquity.

Not the overgrown, bitter giants of commerce, but young romaine with light, sweet juices and tender leaves. I fell in love with romaine in Italy, where only tender heads are sold. The leaves, sweet and juicy, feel soft and velvety to the touch.

Here, young romaine is hard to find. This is where the backyard gardener has a distinct advantage. Farmer's markets sometimes carry the very young leaves.

Select the smallest heads you can find, with bright green, unblemished leaves. If rough, large heads are your only choice, there are a few ways to make them more acceptable. Remove all bruised, withered, browned, and tattered leaves. Discard any leaves with a coarse, pebbled surface. If the ribs are overly large, and dry, discard them too.

sweet torn salad

Salads are a constant in my life. My day isn't complete unless I've eaten at least one.

There are two types of salad—bitter and sweet greens.

For this sweet salad, make sure the lettuces and mint are very fresh. Gently wash the greens and dry on clean tea towels. Handle the leaves with care.

2–3 handfuls small romaine leaves	Extra-virgin olive oil
Handful lamb's lettuce leaves (mâche) or green butter lettuce leaves, optional	1 lemon
	Fine sea salt and black pepper
A few mint leaves	**SERVES 4**

Working over the salad bowl, tear romaine leaves into generous bite-size pieces. Sprinkle in lamb's lettuce leaves, if desired. If using butter lettuce, tear into bite-size pieces over bowl. Tear mint leaves into fragments, scattering them over the top.

Drizzle with olive oil and squeeze lemon over, just enough dressing to barely cloak the leaves, and season with salt and freshly ground pepper. Toss very briefly. Serve without delay.

tasting olive oil in Puglia
(PUGLIA)

It is late one evening, in one of those small,

immaculate towns in Puglia, with deserted streets and houses
that close their eyes to the world. We enter the house and go
down stone steps to the *cantina*, the cellar, where the family's
own olive oil is kept. By the light of a naked bulb, I see liter
wine bottles of olive oil lined up neatly in rows, hand numbered
and dated.

The head of the family inspects the bottles. He selects
one, and we return up the winding stairs and into the kitchen:
another naked bulb and a kitchen table covered with a faded
flowered tablecloth—blue and yellow flowers in a pink grid. The
kitchen is large, plain. He carefully opens the olive oil, and a
perfume escapes through the narrow opening. With total con-
centration and intensity, he pours a trickle of oil onto a piece
of coarse, golden bread.

The olive oil, the most perfect and poignant I've ever had,
tastes fruity, nutty, full-flavored, yet light as a feather on the
tongue. The color: a lapidary, luminescent golden green.

The olives come from the family's small, seven-acre grove

of centuries-old olive trees; they are organically grown and ground in an ancient stone press. And the olive oil we are tasting, he explains, comes from the latest harvest, which was a truly exceptional one.

This oil, its freshness, the pride in the eyes of my host, the modest kitchen, the humble house, the dedication to the land and his intimate connection to it, made me think that, in a sense, he, too, must have sprung directly from the red clay soil, just like the gnarled and twisted olive trees with their pewter-green leaves that shimmer in the wild wind.

(PuGLIA)

arugula salad

Arugula has a distinct and compelling flavor—nutty, pungent, and peppery. I enjoy it straight-up, with just a trickle of fruity olive oil and good sea salt.

Delicious served with a plate of paper-thin slices of bresaola and a chunk of bread.

Small arugula leaves, stem ends trimmed	Fine sea salt
Extra-virgin olive oil	**SERVES 1**

Place arugula leaves in a salad bowl. Drizzle with olive oil and season with salt. Toss briefly. Correct seasonings, if necessary.

spring tonic salad

Since dandelions are one of the first greens to announce the coming of spring, this salad—with dandelions and watercress, sprinkled with an abundance of chopped chives, and hiding a crust of garlic-rubbed bread—makes a fitting springtime offering.

Cultivated dandelion greens are popping up in markets. Look for small, tender leaves no longer than 6 inches; larger leaves are too tough for salad.

Watercress has always been around, waiting patiently to be rediscovered. Select dark green leaves without a trace of yellow. Once picked, watercress has a short life, so any yellowing means the greens are already in decline.

$1/4$ pound tender young dandelion greens

$1/4$ pound, about 1 big bunch, fresh dark green watercress

Chunk of dried country bread

1 garlic clove, peeled

1 bunch chives

3 tablespoons extra-virgin olive oil

1 tablespoon imported red wine vinegar

Fine sea salt

SERVES 4

Cut dandelion greens into very short lengths. Snap off tough stems from watercress. Place greens in a serving bowl.

Rub bread with cut garlic clove. Bury bread in leaves. Use scissors to snip chives over salad. Drizzle with olive oil and vinegar, and season with salt. Toss well.

what is lamb's lettuce?

Lamb's lettuce—also called lamb's tongue lettuce, corn salad, or field salad—is a mild, succulent green with small spoon-shaped leaves. In America, it is often referred to by its French name, mâche. A wild plant that thrives in fields and pastures, lamb's lettuce is also cultivated—with different varieties grown in various seasons.

Lamb's lettuce is known in Italy as valerianella, but also, depending on the region, dolcetta, gallinella, gallinetta, soncino, agnellino, and pasqualina, to name a few! It is traditionally eaten at Eastertime, since that is when this green springs spontaneously from the earth.

I'm very fond of lamb's lettuce and believe it deserves a wider audience. As with all young salad greens, lamb's lettuce, once cut, does require a certain amount of tender loving care.

However, because it grows in rosette clusters and because of its somewhat meaty, succulent character, lamb's lettuce is slightly sturdier than some of the more fragile cut leaves.

Look for lamb's lettuce that is springy and bright green; it holds its freshness longer if sold in its rosette clusters with a little of the root attached. Use within a day or two. Wrap the rosettes (with roots) in a damp tea towel to keep the leaves moist and juicy. Wash gently. Pluck the leaves from the central stem or serve in small clusters after trimming root end.

Add lamb's lettuce to any mix of tender sweet lettuces. Or serve it on its own, in order to truly savor its unique flavor and texture. Try it with tender hard-cooked eggs (see page 106) or very fresh mozzarella. A few drops of walnut oil in a simple dressing points up the slightly nutty taste found in the leaves.

boiled eggs and the five o'clock shadow

The term "hard-boiled" is a misnomer, since boiled eggs are only good when "tender-boiled." We've all seen that dark, unsightly five o'clock shadow that eggs acquire when over-cooked.

It is better to undercook eggs slightly rather than eat them in that dreadful state—dry, crumbly pale yolk, egg whites as rigid as rubber, the egg smelling of sulphur.

To boil an egg properly, here's the method that works best for me: Start the egg or eggs in cold water to cover generously. Slowly bring water to a boil, then gently simmer eggs for 9 to 10 minutes. Drain. Place in a bowl under cold running water until shells feel cool to the touch.

Crack shell by tapping lightly all over egg, then peel. The egg will emerge with a moist, vivid orange yolk cradled in tender but firm egg white.

lamb's lettuce with tender egg

Lamb's lettuce, also called mâche, is a spontaneous springtime offering from nature.

Eggs are an important part of many spring religious rituals, representing the earth's seasonal rebirth after the death experienced in winter when the earth turns cold and lifeless.

Pairing lamb's lettuce with tender boiled eggs makes both symbolic and culinary sense: Both are mild and tender, and both are emblematic of spring. A bed of the succulent, spoon-shaped leaves provides a lovely cushion for the eggs.

If lamb's lettuce is not available, use very fresh, velvety green butter lettuce or limestone lettuce.

1 tablespoon extra-virgin olive oil

2 teaspoons red wine vinegar

1/2 teaspoon prepared Dijon-style mustard

Fine sea salt and black pepper

2 handfuls lamb's lettuce, tender leaves either detached or left in little clusters

2 eggs, preferably organic, boiled until just firm

SERVES 2

Beat together with a fork olive oil, vinegar, and mustard, and season with salt and freshly ground pepper to taste.

Place salad greens on two plates. Peel each egg and cut in half. Nestle egg halves into greens. Drizzle dressing over greens and eggs. Season eggs with extra salt and coarsely ground pepper.

It was not long before our chevalier began to draw large profits from his skill. He fabricated the salad at banquets, at ten guineas apiece. That still would be respectable pay. He was very likely the highest-paid saladier that ever lived. Sometimes, going by his own coach, he performed three ceremonies a night. The sacred wooden bowl, oiled and shining in the candlelight, he approached with dignity, in the punctilio of court costume, with periwig and sword. Romaine was already procurable. The chevalier cast into the leaves the adjuncts of squash buds, tarragon, basil, green tomatoes, finely sliced leeks and wild garlic, nasturtium leaves, heavy olive oil. The salt and peppercorns he pounded with a silver mallet. The vinegar was from Burgundy that had been superlative to begin with, and costlier than in its initial glory.

Chef's holiday, Idwal Jones, 1952
(IDWAL)

purslane

Purslane looks like a miniature jade plant, but grows close to the ground. It has plump, succulent leaves and tender pink stems that taste lightly lemony-tart; all of the plant is edible, including the blossoms. Purslane grows wild, but it is also cultivated.

Its tremendous staying power gives purslane a great advantage over most other salad greens: Once picked, it remains fresh and vital for up to a week; after dressing, purslane continues to be remarkably resilient for hours.

Look for purslane in farmer's markets or markets catering to people from the Mediterranean or Mexico. Or see if you can spot it growing wild in the backyard. A sad reminder: Don't pick purslane if the yard has been sprayed.

damiana's purslane salad

I've loved purslane ever since I was a little girl and my grandmother collected it growing wild in the garden. I started looking for the succulent leaves and tender pink stems myself, so I could nibble on them or make little salads. Not your typical childhood snack!

3 cups roughly chopped purslane, leaves and tender stems only

1 tomato, cut into small chunks

Paper-thin slices red onion

2 tablespoons extra-virgin olive oil

2 tablespoons red wine vinegar

Fine sea salt and black pepper

SERVES 2 TO 4

In a salad bowl, combine purslane, tomato, and red onion. Drizzle with olive oil and vinegar, and season with salt and freshly ground pepper. Toss and correct seasonings.

summer salad

Young peas and carrots, tiny new onions with pearly white bulbs and green tops are added raw, in all their youthful dewiness, to tender lettuces and colorful miniature tomatoes in a salad that celebrates summer's arrival.

About 4 cups sweet lettuce leaves, such as oak leaf, romaine, or velvety butter lettuce

A few sorrel leaves or watercress sprigs

3 new boiling onions with greens still attached

6 ounces unshelled peas, a little less than 1/2 cup shelled

4 small carrots, each 4 to 5 inches long

12 cherry or pear tomatoes (red, yellow, orange, green, striped— just one kind or a mix)

1 small garlic clove, peeled and crushed to a paste

1 teaspoon Dijon mustard

3 tablespoons extra-virgin olive oil

3 tablespoons fresh lemon juice

Fine sea salt and black pepper

SERVES 4

Leave small leaves whole. Tear the larger leaves into bite-size pieces. If using watercress, break off the coarse stems, leaving only the tender top sprigs. Thinly slice the onions. Shell the peas. Peel the carrots and cut into slivers. Cut the tomatoes in half.

In a salad bowl, use a fork to stir together the garlic and mustard. Add the olive oil and lemon, and beat lightly with a fork, adding salt and freshly ground pepper to taste.

Add the prepared ingredients to the salad bowl and toss. Adjust seasonings as needed.

watercress

In America long ago, watercress was collected along the banks of brooks and streams. It was much appreciated for its lively, peppery flavor and tender leaves. Watercress appeared in salads quite regularly in the late 1800s and is still popular today in its cultivated form.

Once picked, watercress withers and yellows very quickly. Select watercress with bright green, unblemished leaves. Do not purchase if any signs of yellowing are present—once it starts to go, it goes very quickly.

Plan to use watercress the same day it is picked, or no later than the next day. To keep it fresh and sprightly, trim a little off the stem ends and immerse it in a glass of water. Cover with a plastic bag and keep in a cool place or refrigerate.

watercress with horseradish bread crumbs

Peppery watercress and hot-sweet horseradish are dynamic, volatile ingredients. Adding buttery bread crumbs tames some of that dynamism, just enough to let the freshness and sweetness emerge.

Since horseradish can be quite fibrous, which makes grating it a struggle, I first make sure the horseradish is firm and fresh. Then I use a zester to finely shred the thin strands instead of grating the entire root.

1 teaspoon unsalted butter

$1/4$ cup coarse whole-grain bread crumbs

1 teaspoon finely shredded and chopped fresh horseradish

1 bunch bright green watercress, coarse stems trimmed

2 handfuls assorted sweet lettuce leaves

2 tablespoons extra-virgin olive oil

1 tablespoon red wine vinegar

Fine sea salt and black pepper

SERVES 4

Melt butter in a small sauté pan. Add bread crumbs and stir over medium heat until crisp and a rich golden brown. Transfer to a small bowl. Add horseradish to bread crumbs and stir.

Place salad greens in a serving bowl. Drizzle with olive oil and vinegar, season with salt and freshly ground pepper, and gently toss. Sprinkle with bread crumbs, toss again, and serve.

julius caesar salad

What to use in Caesar salad now that raw egg yolks are suspect? My version replaces the egg yolk with mascarpone—a real advance in my opinion, since I was never a fan of raw eggs.

The dressing is creamy, lemony, and tangy, with lots of freshly grated Parmesan cheese—just like in a classic Caesar salad.

Try to find young heads of romaine lettuce at a farmer's market. The results are truly memorable.

1 medium garlic clove, peeled and crushed to a paste

3 anchovies, crushed to a paste, optional

2 tablespoons lemon juice

2 tablespoons extra-virgin olive oil

3 tablespoons mascarpone

Fine sea salt and black pepper

3 tablespoons freshly grated Parmesan cheese, plus 1 tablespoon for sprinkling over top

1 head tender romaine lettuce, washed, dried, and torn into bite-size pieces

1½ cups bite-size toasted bread cubes

SERVES 2 TO 4

Combine garlic, anchovies, lemon juice, and olive oil in a small bowl and beat lightly with a fork. Add mascarpone and salt and pepper to taste. Stir until smooth.

Toss romaine with dressing until leaves are lightly coated. Top with bread cubes and grind abundant black pepper over salad. Toss briefly. If desired, sprinkle additional tablespoon of grated cheese over top before serving.

Eat the core of the lettuce—it has sweet juices, a light mineral tang, and a nice crunch. Even gigantic, overgrown super-market romaine has a tasty core. Just trim a little off the surface before eating it.

don't throw it away.

avocados

If you think that avocados first appeared in California during the "avocado and sprouts" sixties, you may be surprised to learn that they have been a part of California agriculture since the first recorded planting in 1848.

For an all-too-brief time I lived in Ventura County, just below Santa Barbara, on the Pacific Ocean—an area that geographically parallels the Mediterranean.

I would often take long walks in the hills, along narrow streets lined with old Spanish-style homes surrounded with lemon and orange trees, quince and fig, and an amazing variety of avocado trees, with green, purple, maroon, and jet black fruits. Usually, I would return home with one or another type of avocado in my pocket.

There was a tree up the hill from my house that produced hundreds of tiny, black-skinned, teardrop-shaped avocados with miniature pits no bigger than an almond and smooth, rich flesh.

Down the street grew a Nabal avocado tree with big, round, grapefruit-size avocados—green-skinned when ripe and with beautiful green-gold, buttery-tasting flesh. And there were Mac Arthur avocados, shaped like large gourds, also green when ripe, with a thin, delicate peel and nutty-tasting flesh.

Along the coast and up into the hills were acres and acres of Hass avocados whose thick, coarsely pebbled skin, black as night when ripe, hides a rich, suave flesh.

In addition, there were Fuertes, Bacon, and Pinkerton avocados—all thriving in the Mediterranean-type climate.

I grew up loving avocados (there were orchards in the San Gabriel Valley town where I was raised), so I felt right at home in Ventura County, living surrounded by avocado trees in the hills above the Pacific Ocean.

avocado with abundant cilantro

Tender romaine leaves and an entire bunch of aromatic cilantro make a soft, glowingly verdant, cushion for lush avocado. Cilantro leaves are used here as a fragrant salad green rather than just as an herbal nuance.

2–3 small heads or 1 medium head romaine lettuce	5 tablespoons lime juice
1 bunch cilantro (fresh coriander)	2 tablespoons extra-virgin olive oil
4 green onions, dark green tops trimmed	Fine sea salt and black pepper
1 large, ripe but firm avocado	**SERVES 2 TO 4**

Remove any tough or bruised outer leaves of romaine. Tear into bite-size pieces. Cut away or pluck off any coarse cilantro stems. Cut green onions into 2-inch lengths and sliver lengthwise into fine julienne. Place prepared ingredients in a salad bowl.

Pit, peel, and dice avocado. Place in a small bowl and gently toss with 1 tablespoon lime juice.

Toss salad with remaining lime juice and olive oil, and season with salt and freshly ground pepper. Spoon diced avocado and juices over top, and toss gently once or twice to distribute the avocado evenly. Taste and correct seasonings, and serve immediately.

salad with almonds and orange perfume

Almonds and oranges grow in all Mediterranean countries, and Spain is no exception. The flavors in this Spanish-inspired salad are extraordinary. The secret? Marinating onion slivers and almonds in a dressing perfumed with orange zest and cumin before tossing with salad greens.

1/4 cup extra-virgin Spanish olive oil or other fruity olive oil

2 tablespoons sherry wine vinegar

Pinch ground cumin

Fine sea salt and black pepper

1 garlic clove, peeled and crushed

1 medium onion, cut into slivers (if desired, soak slivers in cool water first to remove the "bite")

Zest of 1 orange, preferably organic

2 tablespoons coarsely chopped flat-leaf parsley

12 unpeeled freshly toasted almonds, coarsely chopped

4 handfuls tender mixed salad greens, any large leaves torn into bite-size pieces

SERVES 4

In a serving bowl, combine olive oil, vinegar, cumin, salt, and freshly ground pepper, and lightly beat with a fork. Add crushed garlic, onion slivers, orange zest, parsley, and almonds. Stir and set aside for up to 1 hour.

Just before serving, add salad greens and toss well.

the legend of Simonetta

In my cookbooks I like to include at

least one recipe from a little volume I discovered years ago in
an antiquarian bookstore. *A Snob in the Kitchen* was written in
1967 by Simonetta, a famous Italian fashion designer who had
a couture house in Paris during the sixties.

Her photograph on the back of the book jacket shows a
woman simply but dramatically dressed in a leopard-skin tent
coat fastened with big round black buttons, her hair in a
French twist. One hand holds a telephone to her ear, while the
other hand brandishes a cigarette; the backdrop: her elegant
Parisian salon.

I've been fascinated by her life and her culinary sensibilities
since I first leafed through the book's pages. Her simple dishes
always contain a fascinating little twist or turn, and are simultaneously practical, sophisticated, and witty. Adding a recipe of
Simonetta's in the pages of my own books is my homage to
her, and lucky talisman.

salade fatigué

Many of Simonetta's salads, including this one, call for the salad to "season" for an hour before serving. For Simonetta, a salad must be *fatigué*, "tired," to be good; it must be "mixed, beaten, and drunk with its dressing."

In one recipe she directs you to wrap the ingredients in a clean dish towel and whack the bundle against a counter (see Smashed Salad, *Verdura*, page 103) to tenderize the raw ingredients.

Try this salad either way, right after tossing with the dressing, or after an hour of seasoning, when the ingredients have wilted by being "marinated" in the dressing.

1 romaine lettuce heart, torn into small pieces

1 escarole heart, tender white and pale yellow leaves only, cut into small pieces

1 bunch bright green watercress, leaves and tender sprigs only

2 Belgian endives, sliced crosswise

1 small fennel bulb, trimmed and coarsely chopped

10 radishes, thinly sliced

10 button mushrooms, thinly sliced

2 ounces imported Roquefort cheese

6 tablespoons extra-virgin olive oil

5 tablespoons lemon juice

Fine sea salt and freshly ground black pepper

SERVES 4 TO 6

Combine lettuces and vegetables in a big shallow salad bowl. Crumble Roquefort cheese over the top. Drizzle with olive oil and lemon juice, and season with salt and pepper. Toss, taste, and adjust seasonings.

Serve immediately or let rest for an hour before serving.

artichokes stuffed with artichoke salad

I enjoy the leisurely pace of eating whole artichokes leaf by leaf, and the pleasant anticipation of getting closer and closer to the meaty heart.

Almost any kind of composed salad tastes wonderful when spooned into the hollow where the choke once resided. I suggest the following salad, which combines the artichoke's own tender-cooked stem, tangy Pecorino Romano cheese, shiny, rich-tasting black olives, and crisp tomato.

4 fresh medium artichokes

Cut lemon half

Fine sea salt

1/2 cup small, lightly toasted country bread cubes

2 small, ripe but firm tomatoes, cut into small dice

1/2 cup finely diced Pecorino Romano cheese

8 oil-cured olives, pitted and quartered

10 mint leaves

1 teaspoon extra-virgin olive oil

Freshly ground black pepper

Extra-virgin olive oil, lemon juice, lemon wedges

SERVES 4

Trim 1 artichoke at a time, rubbing cut areas with lemon half to prevent blackening. Use a knife to cut across the tops of the leaves to cut away thorny tips. Remove as little of the leaf as possible. Snap back any remaining thorny leaves and pull down to remove coarse fibers. Cut off stems at the base to stabilize artichoke. Trim off dark green exterior of stems.

Arrange artichokes upright in a saucepan just large enough to contain them. Wedge stems into crevices between artichokes. Add water to measure 1/3 up the side of artichokes. Sprinkle with salt. Cover with a tight-fitting lid. Cook at a simmer for 20 minutes, or until artichoke heart is just tender when tested with a thin wooden skewer. Lift artichokes and stems out of water and let cool. Cook down juices a little to concentrate flavor. Spoon juices into cooling artichokes.

Cut stems into small pieces. Combine stems with bread cubes, tomatoes, cheese, and olives. Tear mint leaves over salad. Season with a little olive oil, lemon juice, salt, and pepper. Toss gently.

Gently spread open leaves to reveal choke. Pull out choke with fingers or use a teaspoon to scrape it out carefully, removing as little of the heart as possible.

Spoon salad into artichokes. Drizzle more olive oil and lemon juice over opened leaves, and season with a little salt. Serve with lemon wedges, large napkins, and a bowl for the scraped leaves.

artichokes sir francis rose

Inspiration for this recipe comes from the ever-fascinating *Alice B. Toklas Cookbook*. Featured are three of my favorite ingredients in the whole wide world—artichokes, almonds, and lemons, with a touch of honey in the dressing.

And who is Sir Francis Rose? An artist and author whose name lives on, as does his recipe, in that extraordinary cookbook-cum-memoir and social history.

½ lemon	2 tablespoons lemon juice
3 large, fresh artichokes with long stems	2 teaspoons honey
Fine sea salt	1 lemon, organic if possible
¼ cup raw, unpeeled almonds	
3 tablespoons extra-virgin olive oil	**SERVES 2 TO 3**

Squeeze the lemon half into a big bowl of cold water. Use squeezed lemon to rub cut portions of artichoke as you work. Cut off artichoke stem and trim away tough outer fibers. Cut stem into short sections and place in lemon water. Cut away tops of leaves to just above the heart. Trim away all dark green areas on base of heart. Cut in quarters and cut away choke. Plunge artichoke pieces into lemon water. Repeat with remaining artichokes.

Cook artichokes in a little salted water until they are just tender and a little resistant when pierced with a thin wooden skewer. Drain and let cool. Cut each artichoke quarter in half.

Toast almonds in just enough olive oil to lightly coat the bottom of a small sauté pan. When almonds are very fragrant, transfer to paper towels and sprinkle with salt. Coarsely chop when cool.

Place artichokes and almonds in a serving bowl. Drizzle with olive oil, lemon juice, and honey, and season with salt. Use a zester to make fine, long strands of lemon zest and use the entire lemon. Add zest to the bowl and toss well but gently.

beautiful vegetables

The salad can be served right away. Or let the salad rest for an hour or so to allow flavors to develop. You can even make it in the morning and serve it that evening. In either case, add toasted almonds just before serving. Best eaten at room temperature.

The artichoke stem certainly ranks as one of the great hidden treasures in the plant kingdom. If you enjoy the flavor and texture of the heart, you will be thrilled to discover that the stem, when well trimmed of any tough outside fibers, is tender and fleshy.

Add the stem to any cooked artichoke dish or to dishes that benefit from the flavor of artichoke. When the artichoke is very tender, the peeled stem is good eaten raw (the flavor can be intensely herbal and pleasingly bitter).

don't throw it away.

marinated cherry tomatoes and little white onions

This old-fashioned dish just calls out to be served on the porch on a hot lazy summer's day or taken along on a picnic and enjoyed under a shady tree.

The red and gold cherry tomatoes and tender white boiling onions, which echo the shape and size of the tomatoes, become rich and aromatic after resting in a dressing flavored with dried mustard and abundant fresh dill. Serve this dish along with good country bread to sop up the tomato juices. Set out some cold beer, and let the afternoon just drift away.

1/2 pound small boiling onions, about 2 cups	Fine sea salt and coarsely ground black pepper
3/4 pound red and 3/4 pound yellow cherry or plum tomatoes, about 4 cups total	1/4 cup chopped dill
	1/2 teaspoon finely chopped lemon zest
1/4 cup extra-virgin olive oil	
2 tablespoons red wine vinegar	
1/2 teaspoon dry mustard	**SERVES 4 TO 6**

Blanch onions in boiling water for 2 to 3 minutes. When cool enough to handle, trim stem and root ends and slip off peels. Drain. Return onions to boiling salted water for about 5 minutes, or until just tender. Cut onions in half lengthwise and place in a bowl.

Remove stems and cut tomatoes in half lengthwise. Add to bowl.

Place tomatoes and onions in a big bowl. Combine remaining ingredients in a small bowl and beat lightly with a fork. Pour over vegetables and toss very gently.

Marinate for 1 to 2 hours at room temperature before serving.

beet salad with bright pepper topping

While most often associated with winter, along with other root vegetables, beets grow all year round. They taste especially good in summer. In any season, look for leafy green tops, an indication the roots have just been pulled from the earth.

To turn beets into a late-summer salad, spoon a colorful, crunchy topping of roasted red and yellow peppers, capers, and chopped pickles over the top. The contrast of sugary sweet beets and piquant topping makes this salad hard to resist.

8 small or 4 medium beets	3 tablespoons extra-virgin olive oil
2 bell peppers, 1 red, 1 yellow	2 tablespoons red wine vinegar
2 garlic cloves, peeled and finely chopped	Fine sea salt
1 tablespoon capers	Freshly ground black pepper
6 cornichons or 1 small regular dill pickle, chopped	
15 basil leaves, chopped	**SERVES 3 TO 4**

Boil beets in abundant lightly salted water until just tender. Test with a thin wooden skewer; it should meet with just a hint of resistance.

Drain beets when tender but firm, and cool under cold running water. Peel beets and cut into small chunks.

Meanwhile, roast bell peppers over gas burners, under the broiler, or over a charcoal grill. Peel. Remove core and seeds, and cut away white membranes. Cut peppers into $1/2$-inch squares.

Place peppers in a bowl, and combine with garlic, capers, pickles, and basil. Add olive oil and vinegar, and season with salt and pepper. Toss well. This mixture can be made in advance and rest for several hours if necessary.

Place beets on a platter and spoon pepper mixture over the top.

old-fashioned potato and nasturtium salad

Young nasturtium leaves add a peppery bite to this turn-of-the-century-America potato salad.

Nasturtiums are easy to grow and very pretty; the blossoms unfold in shades of gold, cherry-red, orange, pale butter, and deep crimson; the saucer-shaped leaves cast cool green shadows in the garden.

And in a garden is where I see this potato salad being served, mounded on an antique platter with a floral border, and garlanded with nasturtium leaves and flowers.

If nasturtiums are not available, watercress leaves, a close relative, make an excellent substitute.

1½ pounds new potatoes, about 6 medium-small of even size

Fine sea salt

2–3 cups loosely packed nasturtium greens, small and tender leaves and stems only

½ cup chopped natural dill pickles (see Note)

2 heaping tablespoons capers or pickled nasturtium buds

1 small garlic clove, peeled and finely chopped

5 tablespoons extra-virgin olive oil

4 tablespoons red wine vinegar

Freshly ground black pepper

5 sprigs flat-leaf parsley, leaves finely chopped

Nasturtium petals

SERVES 6

Simmer potatoes for about 20 minutes in salted water to cover by 2 inches. Test with a small, sharp knife or bamboo skewer, and when potatoes are just tender, drain and let cool a little.

Peel potatoes and cut into neat, fairly small dice (this allows the dressing to be absorbed more fully into the potatoes—important since potatoes are mild).

Chop nasturtium leaves and stems.

Place potatoes and nasturtium greens in a large bowl along with pickles, capers, and garlic. Add olive oil, vinegar, and salt and pepper to taste. Toss gently, taking care not to crush the potatoes.

Mound potato salad on a serving plate and sprinkle with parsley. Use scissors to cut nasturtium petals into strips, working directly over the salad and letting them cascade over the top.

Note: No self-respecting old-fashioned potato salad would contain anything other than a natural pickle —like the home-cured ones that once lined kitchen pantry shelves. Select pickles free of preservatives and artificial coloring.

Always save the leafy green tops of beets, turnips, carrots, parsley root, celery root, and other root vegetables. Cook tops in a little lightly salted boiling water. Eat the greens and drink the broth, or use it to flavor soups.

don't throw it away.

lentil salad with spring herbs

A garden's worth of young spring herbs lend their perfume to this piquant lentil salad. A lovely garnish is a wreath of herb sprigs or edible flowers.

Try using French green lentils, as they hold their shape well when cooked. Brown lentils, which are just as delicious as the green ones, must be watched carefully so they do not overcook.

1½ cups French green lentils or brown lentils

Fine sea salt

6 tablespoons extra-virgin olive oil, plus 1 tablespoon

4 tablespoons red wine vinegar, plus 1 teaspoon

Black pepper

1 garlic clove, peeled and finely chopped

2 tablespoons capers

3 tablespoons chopped natural dill pickles

6 tablespoons chopped flat-leaf parsley

2 tablespoons each chopped chives and chopped tarragon

2 big handfuls mixed tender lettuce leaves

SERVES 4 TO 6

Wash lentils. Place in saucepan and cover with a generous amount of water. Add ½ teaspoon salt and bring to a boil. Cook lentils at a steady simmer until tender but slightly resistant, 20 to 25 minutes. Drain well. If using brown lentils, cook for 10 to 15 minutes and drain when just tender.

Toss lentils with olive oil, vinegar, salt, and freshly ground pepper to taste. Add garlic, capers, pickles, and herbs. Toss again and correct seasonings. Let salad rest for 1 to 2 hours. Taste salad and correct seasonings, adding more oil, vinegar, salt, or pepper if needed.

Toss lettuces with remaining tablespoon of olive oil and teaspoon of vinegar. Season with salt and pepper. Arrange on a round platter and mound the lentil salad in the center. If desired, garnish with herb sprigs or edible flowers.

strong salads.

notes on chopping herbs

I can't emphasize enough the importance of working with herbs that are truly fresh—just-picked is the ideal, since herbs lose their strength and sparkle very quickly.

To get the most from your herbs, I suggest the following.

1.
Grow the herbs yourself or select bright, true-colored bouncy leaves that have not been exposed to excessive moisture.

2.
Wash gently and dry the leaves completely before chopping.

3.
Work on a bone-dry cutting board.

4.
Use a sharp knife.

5.
Don't overchop the herbs; work efficiently, using a minimum of strokes.

Water destroys the perfume of the herbs by diluting their essential oils; a wet, green-stained cutting board is a sign of lost flavor and aroma.

Bruising herbs by overchopping or chopping with a dull knife causes volatile oils that carry fragrance and flavor not only to dissipate, but to alter in a negative way.

to keep basil sprigs fresh

Plan to use basil within a day or two of purchase. Trim a little off the stem ends and place the basil sprigs in a glass of water. Keep the leaves well above the water level; wet basil turns black and the sweet odor turns foul. Place glass in a cool part of the kitchen or the refrigerator.

chopped salad

A colorful, crunchy main-dish salad—light and refreshing in hot weather but substantial enough that you won't walk away hungry. A salad to live on all summer long.

1 head romaine lettuce, washed and thoroughly dried

2 medium tomatoes, about 1 pound, cored and diced

1 large yellow bell pepper, cored, seeded, and diced

1/2 cup finely diced red onion

1–1 1/2 cups cooked chick peas

10 oil-cured black olives, pitted and coarsely chopped

8 ounces fresh mozzarella, drained on a folded tea towel, cut into small dice, about 1 cup

1 small bunch basil

4 tablespoons extra-virgin olive oil

2 tablespoons red wine vinegar

1 tablespoon balsamic vinegar

Fine sea salt and black pepper

SERVES 2 TO 3

Working on a very dry cutting board with very dry lettuce, stack romaine leaves and cut across into thin strips. Turn the strips as a mass, then chop crosswise into small pieces.

Place romaine in a large serving bowl and add all the prepared vegetables, chick peas, black olives, and mozzarella. Coarsely chop basil leaves or tear into large fragments and add to salad. Toss gently.

Drizzle olive oil and vinegars over salad. Season with salt and freshly ground pepper to taste. Toss gently but well, correcting seasonings if necessary.

pure panin

133.

how to make a great panino

We are a sandwich-eating society. Our coin of the realm is the sandwich, available in every coffee shop, diner, and fast-food emporium. So, why not treat the sandwich with respect and turn it into a real food, as good for us as it is good to eat?

When made properly with finely crafted bread and carefully chosen ingredients, and keeping freshness and quality in mind, we can be proud of our sandwich tradition.

So, whether you call it a panino or a sandwich, the following rules apply!

1.
Don't assume that all sandwiches must contain either cheese or meat.

2.
Do think in terms of sandwiches with a vegetable filling, such as Vinegared Eggplant Panino on page 143.

3.
Don't automatically add sliced tomatoes and lettuce to all sandwiches. Do use ripe tomatoes or tender lettuces as fillings on their own.

4.
Don't automatically add mustard and mayonnaise to sandwiches.

5.
Do use a little olive oil, lemon juice, or vinegar to moisten and flavor sandwiches. Or try a black or green olive pesto or an herb pesto as a spread.

6.
Various savory condiments make extraordinary panini fillings. Spoon some eggplant and pear caponata into a roll for a delicious, satisfying lunch. Homemade chunky artichoke spread, layered between slices of bread, is equally fine-tasting. (See my book *Verdura* for recipes for both.)

7.

Don't used packaged, plastic-wrapped, presliced bread. Buy whole loaves from bread bakeries or from ethnic markets. Middle Eastern, Russian, and German markets often carry excellent breads made by small-scale ethnic bakeries. The breads must be touched by the baker's hand, be free of preservatives and other additives, and contain wholesome, nutritious ingredients.

8.

Do slice the loaves with a good bread knife. A little variation in the slices adds a human dimension to a sandwich and contributes to its power to nourish.

9.

Don't pile too many ingredients into a sandwich. Exercise some restraint. Consider using only one ingredient, or limit your selection to a choice few. Eating is more satisfying when each ingredient can be savored.

10.

If possible, don't refrigerate sandwiches after assembling. Most don't require refrigeration if eaten within an hour or so. Chilling dulls the fresh flavors of many ingredients, even when brought back to room temperature. The flavor and feel of bread suffer terribly when eaten refrigerator-cold.

11.

Don't pack sandwiches in plastic bags, such as those with Ziploc tops, or plastic wrap.

12.

Do use fresh white cotton napkins or clean white tea towels, brown paper, or wax paper. These materials allow the sandwich to breathe and help create a more natural eating experience.

Don't ever throw away good dried bread. Bread has many lives and many uses. When it is bone-dry, put it in paper bags and store in a dry place.

As needed, crush dried bread with a mortar and pestle or in a hand-cranked cheese grater and use the crumbs instead of flour to line a baking dish, to coat vegetables for frying, or to toast and sprinkle over pasta.

Add chunks of dried bread to fortify soups and salads, or rub a ripe tomato half into the bread to soften and flavor it, sprinkle with salt and dried oregano, and eat as a snack.

new garlic/dried garlic

Garlic freshly pulled from the earth before it is dried for storage has a moist and pearly white skin; the cloves are sweet and juicy, unblemished and innocent as a newborn baby. Look for it in farmer's markets or specialty produce markets in late spring or early summer.

Dried garlic is more assertive but should always be moist and sweet. But if the garlic is bruised or yellowing, if the cloves feel soft instead of firm, if the cloves look dry or withered, it will taste harsh. I don't know for sure if the green shoot sometimes found in a clove means that the garlic is bitter, but many people claim that this is the case. Usually, if I add raw garlic to a salad, I take the green shoot out, and when I cook with garlic, I leave it in.

Just remember, careful selection of garlic is one of the underpinnings of good cooking.

tiny garlic sandwiches

Imagine a sandwich of transparent slivers of fresh, sweet garlic on small, thin rounds of sturdy bread. Moistened with olive oil or a little sweet butter and with an herb leaf slipped between the bread slices, this sandwich makes a good companion for soups or salads, or it can be eaten as an afternoon snack with a cool glass of water.

Extra-virgin olive oil or unsalted butter

2 slices high-quality baguette, thinly sliced on the diagonal

1 fresh garlic clove, peeled and sliced paper-thin

Fine sea salt and black pepper

A few tender herb leaves, such as basil, mint, chives, or flat-leaf parsley

MAKES 1

Drizzle with olive oil or lightly butter bread. Arrange garlic slices on 1 bread slice and sprinkle lightly with salt and freshly ground pepper. Sprinkle with a few herb leaves or cut chives. Cover with remaining bread slice and press down to bind ingredients.

green olive panino

As a child, and following my mother's example, I would make myself green olive sandwiches. What is a green olive sandwich? Simply the meat of green olives between slices of bread.

Green olives have an excitingly tart and salty edge to their flavor. My grandmother used to add celery and garlic to the cracked green olives she cured—the ones from our backyard olive tree.

I can taste this sandwich in my mind—fragrant with the herbal scent of celery leaves, with the warm heat of garlic on my tongue, and the feel of firm olive flesh between my teeth.

Either buy olives seasoned with garlic and celery from a high-quality source or make your own (see page 42 in my book *Verdura*).

Green olives flavored with celery and garlic	
2 slices rustic bread	**MAKES 1**

If the olives were cracked before curing, the flesh will easily come away from the pit with the aid of a paring knife. Otherwise, use a knife to cut strips of flesh off the pit. Arrange the olive meat and a little of the olive seasonings on a slice of bread. Cover with remaining bread slice.

pioneer spirit versus community spirit

Don't feel you have to do it all yourself. We are no longer pioneers out in the remote wilderness of America. In Europe tradition has always been communal.

There was a communal oven where everyone baked bread, or a bread baker who supplied the town with its daily loaves. Fancy pastries have always been the domain of pastry chefs and are rarely made at home. Cheese makers and sausage makers, too, are respected craftspeople.

In Europe and many other parts of the world, there is no shame associated with buying fresh-baked bread. And when presenting a beautiful sweet creation, there is no need for subterfuge, for the pretense of having prepared it yourself.

Supporting artisanal producers is important. For example, the life of a bread baker is a difficult one—early hours, hot ovens. But the work is done out of love and passion, and we should feel gratitude when tasting the fruits of that labor.

panino di papà

This was my father's panino. He made it with very fresh lean ricotta, which he loved since his Sicilian boyhood, and with nutritious, high-protein walnuts.

2–3 tablespoons fresh ricotta, drained first if very moist	A few walnut meats
2 slices rustic whole grain bread	**MAKES 1**

Spread ricotta on 1 slice of bread, stopping short about ½ inch from edge. Sprinkle with walnuts. Cover with remaining bread.

bread and chocolate memories

Ever since the publication of *panini, bruschetta, crostini*, which showed a bittersweet chocolate sandwich on the cover, many people have shared with me their bread and chocolate memories. Many of these stories come from the children of Europeans, now all grown-up and nostalgic.

The most surprising story, however, came from my mother-in-law. Upon seeing the cover of my book for the first time, she instantly remembered a long-forgotten sandwich she ate on a hot and dusty car trip across the Texas plains in 1947.

The Hershey sandwich was listed on the menu of the small, ramshackle roadside café where they stopped for lunch. She was curious about what this strange offering might be. It was a Hershey bar slapped between two slices of Wonder Bread and grilled on an old-fashioned sandwich grill!

tomato and oregano panino

One of my favorite childhood treats was a simple tomato sandwich, which I sprinkled with dried oregano and salt, and a few drops of red wine vinegar.

It tasted cool and refreshing, and nicely pungent, even when made with supermarket bread. It was the strong, wild perfume of our backyard dried oregano along with ripe tomatoes that made the sandwich taste good, in spite of the dreadful bread.

In the heat of summer, a tomato sandwich is as refreshing now as it was then. These days, the bread I use is the real thing, coarse-textured and nutritious. The tomatoes are organically grown. But the dried oregano remains the same: pungent, floral, and infused with the scent of summer.

1 ripe but firm tomato, sliced	Dried whole-leaf Mediterranean oregano
2 slices rustic bread	
Fine sea salt	
Red wine vinegar	**MAKES 1**

Arrange tomato rounds on 1 slice of bread. Season with salt and a few drops of vinegar. Crush oregano leaves over tomatoes to release scent. Cover with remaining bread slice.

monster mushroom panino

A large, fresh mushroom, whether a portobello, shiitake, or porcini, roasted, grilled or seared, makes a satisfying filling between slices of rustic bread.

Embellished only with thin slivers of garlic before cooking, the mushroom's essence—its light and juicy flesh, its bosky nuances of earth, minerals, fallen leaves—comes through clearly. Sturdy country bread absorbs the thin, exciting juices that flow from the mushroom as you bite into the sandwich.

Serve with a few black olives on the side and a glass of red wine for an earthy and satisfying dinner for one. And don't neglect to make yourself a simple leafy green salad to go with your panino.

1 very large, thick mushroom, portobello, shiitake, or porcini

Thin slivers of peeled garlic

Extra-virgin olive oil

Fine sea salt and black pepper

2 slices rustic bread, about the size of the mushroom

MAKES 1

Wipe mushroom clean with damp tea towel. Trim away entire stem. Make small, shallow cuts in mushroom cap and gently slide in garlic slivers. Brush with olive oil. To cook mushroom cap, grill, roast, or sear in a hot pan on both sides until it just barely begins to soften. Overcooking causes the mushroom to collapse and release its juice, thus compromising its meaty texture.

Meanwhile, toast or grill bread slices. Drizzle with a few drops of olive oil. Place mushroom cap on one bread slice, season with salt and freshly ground pepper, and cover with remaining bread slice.

vinegared eggplant panino

You'll be astonished at how sweet and light the flavor of eggplant flesh is when it's simply boiled until just tender, then very lightly dressed with olive oil and vinegar.

Initially, it will taste a little sharp from the vinegar, but after several hours, the flavors develop and the vinegar softens. Start with raw red wine vinegar, a natural, living vinegar with a mellow flavor—my vinegar of choice and available at natural food stores—and select a firm eggplant free of bruises and soft spots.

On a hot summer day, the sandwich is particularly refreshing when the filling comes straight out of the refrigerator.

Although there will be enough filling to make several delicious sandwiches, I could very easily, and happily, sit down and eat all the eggplant myself.

One 1-pound eggplant

1 garlic clove, finely chopped

3 tablespoons raw red wine vinegar

1 tablespoon extra-virgin olive oil

1 teaspoon dried Mediterranean oregano, such as Greek oregano

Fine sea salt

2–3 rustic bread rolls

MAKES 2 TO 3

Cut eggplant into medium chunks. Cover with water, add salt, and bring to a boil. As the eggplant cooks, push it down into the water several times, or lay a large Chinese strainer over the top to keep the eggplant immersed.

After 5 to 10 minutes, or when the eggplant is just tender (a thin wooden skewer that meets with no resistance is the test), drain well. Wrap eggplant in several layers of tea towels to absorb excess water and let drain for several hours.

Place eggplant in a bowl and add remaining ingredients, adding salt to taste. Lightly mash eggplant with a fork to help it absorb seasonings. Let mellow for several hours at room temperature or refrigerate for a day or two.

don't be afraid to repeat dishes

In my family we basically ate the same all year round, with a seasonal rotation of dishes: In cool weather, we had broccoli with lemon or wild greens, in summer, a salad of tomato, potato, and green beans. It never occurred to me to grow tired of these dishes. Each time we had them I enjoyed them just as much or even more, like a friendship that grows deeper with the years.

My grandmothers always prepared their specialties. Nonna, my mother's mother, grew up in the lap of luxury in the city of Palermo, and never learned to cook until late in life. Her special dishes were red squash with sugar and red wine vinegar and caponata both of which are famous Palermitani dishes. (See *Cucina Fresca* for Caponata della Nonna, page 146, and *Verdura*, page 65, for Sweet and Sour Red Squash with Mint.) She also prepared elegantly diced potatoes sautéed with rosemary and butter, and risotto with peas, which she learned to make during the years she lived in Verona.

My other grandmother, my father's mother, was a countrywoman from the Madonie Mountains in Sicily. She collected and cooked wild greens, marinated boiled eggplant in olive oil, vinegar and oregano (see page 143), made pasta and broccoli soup.

To this day, these foods sharply recall to me my grandmothers; I can see them at the stove cooking carefully and lovingly, smell the pungency of red wine vinegar or the strong herbal aroma of dried oregano. I can feel their presence when I prepare those dishes in my own kitchen.

So, don't be afraid to repeat dishes. Decide on a few simple signature dishes and serve them again and again to your heart's content—for family and for friends. Remember, the complexity of your cooking or its ceaseless novelty is not the measure of who you are.

tomato and mozzarella "toast"

A "toast" is the Italian version of our grilled cheese sandwich. This one has a layered filling of tomato, mozzarella, and basil—a threesome almost as sacred in Catholic Italy as the Holy Trinity.

Toasted until the bread crisps and the cheese melts to a cream, this tastes sublime with a small glass of cold beer.

2 squares focaccia or other flatbread, not more than 1 inch thick	Fine sea salt and freshly ground black pepper
Extra-virgin olive oil	1 large Roma tomato, ripe but firm, cored and sliced into rounds
1/4 pound fresh mozzarella (1/2 a large ball), thinly sliced and drained on tea towels	4 basil leaves
	MAKES 2

Split focaccia squares horizontally. Drizzle a little olive oil on the inside of all 4 pieces. Arrange mozzarella on bottom half of the bread slices, and season with salt and pepper. Top with tomato rounds and season again. Arrange basil leaves over tomatoes and cover with focaccia tops.

Place sandwiches on a hot grill or in a hot sauté pan and weigh down with a heavy pot or other weights. Grill for a few minutes on one side, and when golden, flip over and grill other side. Sandwiches are ready when cheese melts and bread turns crusty. Serve hot.

afternoon refreshment

Afternoon is the traditional time to stop the tumult of the day for a moment, to rest, reflect, repair, and gently revive oneself. In Italy, it often consists of a stop at a *caffè/bar* or a *pasticceria*, pastry shop, for an espresso and a sweet.

Taking afternoon tea or an espresso/cappuccino need not be reserved for important or special occasions only. I'm convinced that spur-of-the-moment afternoon teatime for one or two tastes best of all when one has improvised a little sandwich with a touch of sweetness, like bread with jam.

joined ladyfingers

For a touch of sweetness, ladyfingers, those delectable light-as-air cookies, make a wonderful ending to a meal. Spread with a thin gloss of good jam, this becomes an elegant little dessert panino. In the afternoon brew yourself a cup of espresso or tea and enjoy a ladyfinger sandwich.

Ladyfingers, homemade or purchased from a high-quality bakery	Preserves, homemade (see pages 286–290) or high-quality purchased variety

If the preserves are very solid, warm them first to soften a little. Gently spread preserves on the flat side of the ladyfinger. Cover with another ladyfinger.

peach sandwich

Sugared sliced peaches on toasted rustic bread makes a sandwich just right for a summer day.

2 slices sturdy rustic bread	1 ripe, fragrant peach, sliced (peeling is optional)
A little unsalted butter	Sugar to taste

Toast the bread slices and, while warm, lightly spread with butter. Arrange peach slices on 1 slice of bread and sprinkle with sugar (amount depends on the sweetness of the peach). Cover with the other bread slice and very gently press down to bind.

bread with toppings

149.

Perfect lemon love.

Some people like the taste of lemon—for me it borders on religion. I've loved the taste of lemons since childhood, when my favorite special meal was lettuce salad dressed with lemon and oil, and thin veal scallops with a squeeze of lemon, prepared especially for me by my mother's sweet, loving hands.

I squeeze lemon over lettuces, beans, vegetables, fresh cheeses; into soups, stews, pastas, and rice; on bread and pizza; on fish and chicken and beef; and on strawberries and fruit salads.

Like a pilgrim, I visit towns in Italy famous for the quality of their lemons. On my desk for the last five years there's been a postcard I bought in Amalfi showing a close-up of big, bumpy-skinned, extraordinary lemons of the Costa Amalfitana, piled into a large basket and strewn with fresh lemon leaves. The basket is perched on a rocky promontory with the blue sea as background.

sicilian bread with lemon

When I was twelve, my family and I went on our first trip to Italy. We stayed for several summer months, part of the time in Zia Gina's elegant Palermo apartment.

One day I became almost insane with the pleasure of the food I was eating. I ate so much golden Sicilian bread—drizzled with fruity olive oil, drenched in sweet lemon juice, and sprinkled with salt—that a doctor had to be called.

He confined me to bed for a few days and, to calm my tummy, restricted my eating to clear broth. I greeted this news with a quiet elation, since the clear amber broth I had spooned into my mouth with a big Italian soup spoon at Zia Rubina's house the day before was one of the best things I'd ever tasted.

Sicilian bread is made from durum, or hard wheat, flour; the crust is embedded with abundant sesame seeds. In America the bread can be found in markets on the East Coast and at artisanal bread bakeries across the country. If this bread is not easily available in your area, I encourage you to make it at home (see page 296).

| Sicilian bread (see Note) | Lemons |
| Extra-virgin olive oil | Fine sea salt |

Slice bread to desired thickness. Drizzle lightly with olive oil and squeeze a generous amount of lemon juice over the top. Season with salt.

Note: Do not grill or toast the bread first. Semolina bread has a dense crumb that easily absorbs the olive oil and lemon juice without becoming overly soft.

children and food

We can learn a great deal about eating from children. They have highly sensitive taste buds and instinctual cravings.

Most very young children love vegetables, but prefer to eat them separately rather than mixed together, and they often prefer to eat them raw. They don't care for any extra flavoring and find pleasure in the simplest, unadorned foods.

Children are more attuned to their body's needs regarding when and how much to eat, rather than society's imposed strictures.

They like to eat with their hands—a very direct way, unspoiled by the taste of metal—even though some societies, including ours, frown on such things.

country garlic bread and grapes

I would advise giving children their garlic by rubbing some energetically over a good crusty piece of country bread, then dripping a bit of olive oil over the slice. This makes an excellent snack for youngsters. I feasted on this all through my childhood. With a bit of salt and a cluster of golden-skinned, sun-warmed grapes, it makes a wonderful lunch.

Maurice Mességué
C'est la Nature Qui a Raison, 1972

grilled bread with goat cheese and honey

Make this for yourself or for a child as an afternoon snack for a chill autumn day. When the walnuts are freshly fallen from the trees, their meat will be sweet and lightly tannic. Get your best honey down from the shelf, to drizzle on top.

1 round fresh goat cheese, sliced from a log	Honey, preferably raw
1 thick slice rustic bread	
Walnut meats from 2 cracked walnuts	**SERVES 1**

Arrange goat cheese on bread and place in a 350° oven. Remove from oven when bread edges are toasted and cheese is warmed through, about 15 minutes. Sprinkle with walnuts and drizzle with a thin thread of honey.

bruschetta

Bruschetta is a thick slice of grilled country bread, rubbed with a freshly cut clove of raw garlic and drizzled with olive oil. It is the original Italian garlic bread.

The following recipes are for bruschetta with simple toppings. Good to eat at a picnic, for lunch or dinner—either preceding another course or as the main course itself—or enjoyed as an afternoon snack.

It is crucial that the bread be authentic, not bleached and stripped, but wholesome, fragrant, sturdy, and glorious.

eating crushed tomato bread

YOU are in the garden making lunch. Heat a grill with natural charcoal. Let your eyes wander through the tomato foliage until you find a big red tomato that is nearly bursting with juice. Pick it and smell the stem end, luxuriate in the lingering green-spice scent left behind by leaves and stem.

Set a piece of bread on the grill and, turning once, grill it until both sides are golden and slightly scorched in places. Cut the tomato in half and rub the cut sides of the tomato firmly into the coarse surface of the bread. Watch as the juices release into the bread and the tomato flesh, fresh and fruity, separates from the peel. All that should remain in your hand is the thin, spent skin of garden tomato. Dribble the bread with olive oil, and scatter sea salt and dried oregano leaves and flowers on top.

Then sit down in a nearby shady spot, breathe in the mingled scents of tomato leaves, earth, and flowers in bloom, and slowly eat the tomato bread.

crushed tomato bread

For this rough-and-ready dish, the bread must be a very sturdy country variety and the best tomato to use is one that grows in your garden. Slow-ripened, plump, and thin-skinned, the tomato's flavor and fragrance expand under the warmth of the sun just as the heat makes our senses expand.

1 large, thick slice country bread	Fine sea salt
1 garlic clove, peeled and cut in half	Dried Mediterranean oregano, such as Greek oregano
Extra-virgin olive oil	
1 very ripe medium tomato	**SERVES 1**

Grill bread on both sides until golden. Rub 1 side with cut sides of garlic and drizzle with olive oil. Cut tomato in half horizontally (to help release juices and flesh). Rub cut sides of tomato energetically into bread until all juice and flesh have been transferred. Drizzle with olive oil, and sprinkle with salt and oregano.

bruschetta with sweet vegetables

Spread it on bread, use it as a pizza topping, eat it from a big spoon—however you choose to enjoy this wonderful mixture of chopped leeks, sweet red pepper, and grated Parmesan cheese—if you make it once, I guarantee you'll make it again. It is easy to prepare, fresh-tasting, and surprisingly rich in flavor.

4 medium leeks, about 1 pound

1 fleshy, deep-red sweet bell pepper, trimmed and seeded

3 tablespoons extra-virgin olive oil

3 tablespoons chopped flat-leaf parsley

Very small pinch hot red pepper flakes

$1/4$ cup freshly grated Parmesan cheese

Fine sea salt and freshly ground black pepper

Rustic bread slices

MAKES 4

Trim leeks to white and very pale yellow portions. Cut in half lengthwise, then thinly slice crosswise. Place in a large colander and run cold water over leeks, tossing with your hands, to expose all pieces to water and remove all traces of grit.

Cut sweet red pepper into thin strips, then cut again crosswise to make small dice.

Heat olive oil in a large sauté pan. Add leeks, red bell pepper, parsley, and hot red pepper flakes. Sauté over medium heat until vegetables are tender. Off heat, stir in Parmesan cheese. Taste and add salt, if needed, and pepper to taste.

Grill or toast about 4 slices of bread. Spread mixture on warm bread and serve.

Note: You can prepare the vegetable mixture even 1 day in advance. It will still taste quite good, although it will have lost that truly fresh sparkle. Gently warm before using.

describe in twenty words or less

It is the color of bitter chocolate and it is shaped like a dirt clod. I've been inhaling its strong perfume deeply, wantonly, and I feel a little lightheaded. I try to capture the elusive scent in words; a scent that is alive, moving and changing every moment.

What does the aroma evoke? Rich earth; garlic; damp, rotting leaves; autumn smoke; and a high, almost sweet note that floats just beyond my grasp. Could it be acorns?

What is this earthy, evasive creature? It is the Italian black truffle.

157.

bruschetta with black truffle

The very earthbound truffle's character is coarse, powerful, slightly rude, and a little funky, leaving its uncivilized, wild scent on anything that brushes against it or gets in its way.

I want a simple wine with my truffle. I want my truffle on crusty, warm-tasting bread, made from grains as unrefined as the truffle itself. And I want to hold the warm bread with its black truffle cargo in my hand so I can bring it close to my nose to greedily breathe in its perfume.

There is no trick to preparing this bruschetta. Just be sure the bread is honest and the truffle is fresh.

1 small black truffle, 1/2 ounce or more

3 tablespoons unsalted butter or extra-virgin olive oil

4 slices coarse rustic bread

MAKES 4

Peel truffle with vegetable peeler. Reserve peels (see Note).

Place truffle and butter or olive oil in a very small baking dish, such as a custard cup, and cover tightly with foil.

Bake at 325° for 30 minutes. Grill or toast bread during the last few minutes of cooking.

Brush bread with butter or oil. Cut truffle into thin (not paper-thin) slices. Place several truffle slices over surface of bread. Serve right away.

Note: The peels are a little coarse-textured but highly aromatic. Place them in a small mason jar, cover with olive oil, close tightly, and refrigerate. After a few weeks you will have truffle-scented oil to drizzle over spaghettini, tender cardoons, braised celery, or warm rice salad.

crostini

Crostini are smaller versions of bruschetta, sliced more thinly, and often toasted in the oven rather than grilled.

The following is a list of toppings that would perfectly cap rounds or squares of crostini.

Avocado Spread (page 58)

Perfumed Tomato Dip (page 59)

Farmer's Cheese with Chives (page 60)

Ricotta Fresca (page 64)

Tabbouleh (page 92)

Marinated eggplant from Vinegared Eggplant Panino (page 143)

Grilled Bread with Goat Cheese and Honey (page 153)

The topping from Bruschetta with Sweet Vegetables (page 156)

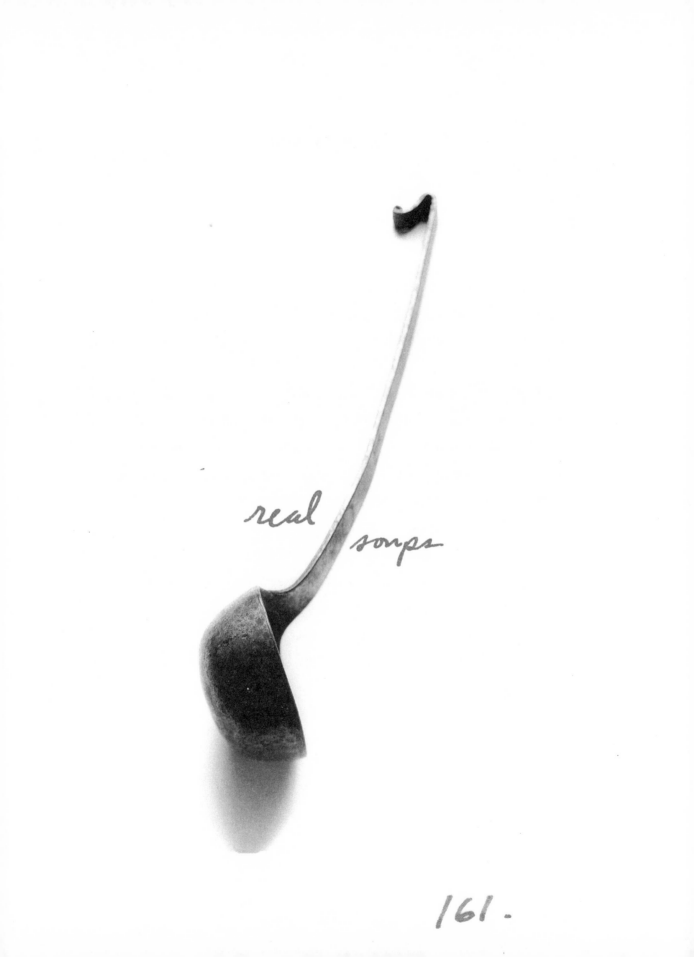

real
soups

161.

water for soup

Water is the most important element in all the recipes that follow. Just as most of the earth's surface is water, and our bodies are mostly water, soup is 90 percent water.

Water is not a neutral ingredient—it can taste good, and it can taste bad.

I strongly recommend pure spring water, which has a sweet mineral flavor, for all the soups in this book.

Most tap water has a chemical taste and smell that not only intrude upon the flavor and perfume of the soup, but also upon the health of those who drink it. The simpler the soup, the more obvious the water's poor quality. And even in more highly flavored soups, the water can severely impair the final product. Foul chemical smells can render soups inedible.

If you balk at using that much bottled water, remember, good soup is worth the very minimal expense of good water.

For the soup pot, you gather from the garden ruffled Swiss chard leaves, and in the market you search for the most luminescent bunch of carrots with the freshest green tops. Why, then, would you subject them to anything but pure water?

I use spring water for all my soup making. The flavor of pure water—alive, clean, of earth, rock, and glinting mineral—is one of the joys of life. Let it contribute its extraordinary properties to the soup pot.

when to serve soup

In many cultures soup is a main dish—satisfying, nourishing, and complete. In our culture, however, soup is all too often relegated to lunch or, if served in the evening, given a diminished role as a prelude to other dishes.

Whether you call it supper or dinner, the last meal of the day is one of the best times to serve soup. Eating light at night is sensible and a kindness to our bodies. After all, most of us are rather sedentary between dinnertime and bedtime.

How does soup become a dinner? If it is a quite hearty soup, it need only be accompanied by good bread, salad—a few tender green leaves or sliced summer tomatoes—and a piece of ripe fruit.

If appetites are highly charged, or the soup is very light, in addition to bread, salad, and fruit offer one or two simply cooked seasonal vegetables. Then, if a bit more substance is needed, have a sliver of frittata, a little prosciutto, or a bowl of olives. Often when I have a simple soup and small salad for supper, I end my meal with fruit and a few almonds or walnuts.

on seasoning soups

The soups that follow take little time to prepare, but short preparation time was not my goal. It is directness of flavor that is important and what I'm after.

If you're tempted to spruce up the recipes because they seem too austere, please try them first as I've presented them. The mineral essence of greens, the lush flavor of freshly harvested winter squash, the bosky quality of mushrooms—when was the last time you tasted them on their own without the usual heavy herb or spice overlay?

three cures.

When I'm not feeling well, or when I want to give my system a rest, I take "The Verdura Cure," my name for an Italian tradition. I learned this "cure" from my mother when I was growing up. It is one of the secrets of Italian good health, not written about in cookbooks but passed down from one generation to the next.

The word *verdura* has several shades of meaning in Italian. It means one vegetable, or vegetables in general. *Verdura* is also used to describe leafy greens for cooking. Again, it can mean one type of green or the entire category of greens. The long list of greens popular in Italy includes escarole, Swiss chard, endive, summer squash leaves cooked as greens, and all those leaves that grow naturally in the Italian countryside: chicory, wild cabbage, highly aromatic and tasty wild fennel greens, arugula, mustard greens, wild beet tops, borage, dandelion, and nettles.

My mother's grandmother used to fast once a month. Instead of eating, she sipped the pot liquor from boiled greens.

The greens were purchased in the early morning. *"Verdurina fresca, verdurina fresca,"* the vendors would sing out—and the housekeeper would signal to them from the balcony to come to the door with baskets full of wild greens they had collected at dawn, the roots still caked with fresh earth.

Once you became a steady client of the forager, he would come at scheduled times to deliver the absolutely freshly picked greens as often as you desired. Whatever was growing wild that month or that season was picked at dawn by the vendors and delivered to their customers by 6:00 in the morning.

The greens were boiled in a large pot of clean, pure, delicious water from natural springs, which in those days just required a turn of the kitchen faucet, until the leaves were falling-apart

165.

tender and the broth was dark and *amarostico,* nicely bitter. No olive oil was added, but sometimes a very discreet pinch of sea salt was used.

Signora Li Mandri, my great-grandmother, whom my mother Antonietta was named after, would drink the hot broth from the boiled greens all day and eat the tender greens plain, sometimes with a few drops of lemon. But it was the broth, she maintained, that contained all the curative powers. She fasted, she said, "to give the digestive system a rest and to cleanse the body." On her day of fasting, my great-grandmother even abstained from drinking espresso—which she considered her greatest sacrifice!

This monthly regimen of fasting, along with extended, vigorous, and purposeful walks throughout the city even during the oven blast of summer heat, kept my great-grandmother strong and vital into her later years. Also, keeping her hair tinted a rich black (using the water in which unripe green walnuts soaked as a natural dye) may also have contributed to her youthful spirit!

the verdura cure

I love to sip this broth all day long when I'm feeling under the weather, in need of a tonic, or when I want to rest my body. It is delicious and invigorating.

Although the greens are "exhausted" after all that boiling, and their goodness has been transferred to the broth, the leaves still taste good, especially if you squeeze some lemon on them.

2 pounds bitter greens, such as endive, mustard greens, dandelion greens, kale, collard greens, or a mix

Spring water to cover greens generously

Pinch sea salt, optional

Lemon juice, optional

Wash greens well by soaking them in a large sinkful of cold water. Let dirt settle to the bottom of the sink and lift out greens without disturbing water. Drain and rinse sink. Repeat 2 or 3 times until no grit or dirt remains in bottom of sink when water is drained.

Cut greens lengthwise in half or in thirds. Place in a large soup pot and cover generously with water. If desired, add a very small pinch of salt. Bring to a boil and simmer until the greens are meltingly tender, and broth darkens and is flavored by the greens.

Sip the broth throughout the day, reheating as needed. Lift out the greens and eat, sprinkled with a few drops of lemon juice if you wish.

gentle flavors

With the present-day emphasis on big, bold, hot, and hotter flavors in food, I often wonder if everyone has forgotten that gentle, subtle flavors are a source of tremendous pleasure, too.

Allow your taste buds to enjoy the delicate vegetal flavor of zucchini blossoms, the light botanical essence of a simple vegetable broth, the sweet juices in a sliver of unadorned raw fennel, the astonishing, pure taste of fresh ricotta.

parsley tonic

After making tabbouleh, you will be left with a mountain of parsley stems. It would be a shame to throw them away, since they possess so much goodness and flavor. Instead, transform the stems into a tonic broth and sip a cup of it.

| Flat-leaf parsley stems | Fine sea salt |
| Spring water | |

Generously cover parsley stems with water. Simmer for an hour or so. Strain, reheat, and season with a bit of salt.

romaine broth/soup

You may want to make this soup the next time your nerves feel jangly! Romaine contains a natural calmative. In Italy romaine is boiled in water, then the broth is given to crying *bambini* to help them sleep.

In this recipe the lettuce leaves remain in the broth, and garlic and bread add flavor and substance. The soup is delicious, but the flavor is gentle rather than strong. And don't expect a lot of liquid. A small amount of broth concentrates the sweet, delicate flavor of romaine.

1 head tender romaine lettuce	Extra-virgin olive oil
1½ cups spring water	Freshly grated Parmesan cheese
Fine sea salt	Freshly ground black pepper
1 garlic clove, peeled and cut in half	
A few small pieces dried rustic bread	**SERVES 2**

Wash romaine, hold leaves in a bunch, and tear them into medium fragments. In a medium soup pot, combine romaine and water. Add salt to taste. Boil lettuce until ribs are tender, about 10 minutes.

Lightly rub cut sides of garlic clove on all sides of bread pieces and place in 2 soup bowls. Drizzle bread with olive oil. Ladle greens and broth over bread. Drizzle with a thin thread of oil, and sprinkle with grated cheese and a touch of coarsely ground pepper.

three broths.

beyond broth as we know it

Broth can easily be made from sources other than meat and fish. The water in which a single plant cooks can make a superb broth—good to use in soups or stews or to sip from a cup or mug.

A broth made from mushrooms simmered in fresh spring water (see page 171), or from a single green, such as escarole; a heap of flat-leaf parsley stems left over from making tabbouleh (see page 92); or from cooking dried beans in a generous amount of sweet water. All these broths are tasty and sustaining.

There is no trick to making broths, and there are no endless lists of ingredients to add, simply pure water into which is transferred a clean, sparkling flavor.

mushroom consomme

This rich, mushroomy, clear amber broth makes a posh first course served in consomme cups, accompanied by tiny hot biscuits, split and enclosing a sliver of cold green herb butter.

Delicious taken in the afternoon as a savory "tea" sipped from a thin porcelain cup, but it tastes every bit as good when drunk from an old beat-up mug.

The mushrooms graciously offer up most of their flavor to the broth. But don't discard them! A drizzle of olive oil and lemon, and a bit of salt and pepper, revive the mushrooms just enough so you can turn them into a little salad if desired.

$1\frac{1}{2}$ pounds brown mushrooms (cremini, field, or Roman mushrooms)

3 dried porcini mushroom slices, well rinsed to remove grit, optional but desirable

6 cups spring water

Fine sea salt

SERVES 4 TO 5

Place brown mushrooms in a colander and briefly run cold water over them, using your hands to gently lift mushrooms so as to expose all sides to water. Wipe mushrooms with a clean old tea towel.

Simmer brown mushrooms, dried porcini mushrooms, if desired, spring water, and salt for 1 to $1\frac{1}{2}$ hours, or until broth is reduced to 4 or 5 cups, depending on desired strength of flavor.

Lift out mushrooms with a large strainer and set aside. Strain broth through 4 layers of dampened cheesecloth in order to trap all remaining particles. Gently reheat broth and serve.

beet and lemon broth

Deeply rich and red, imbued with the sweet mineral, earth essence of beets; this fragrant broth comes alive with a big squeeze of lemon juice just before serving.

Sip this vibrant and tangy beet and lemon broth from a thin cup as an afternoon tonic, or serve it as a bracing consomme at the beginning of a meal.

1 bunch fresh beets, about 4 to 5 medium beets, with leafy green tops

2 medium leeks, tops trimmed, or an onion or a few shallots

A few flat-leaf parsley sprigs

A few sprigs carrot tops, if on hand

6 cups spring water

Fine sea salt

Squeezed lemon juice to taste

MAKES ABOUT 4 CUPS

Completely trim off beet tops and cut away "tails." Reserve leaves for another use. Vigorously scrub beets to remove surface grit. Cut into quarters. Slit leeks vertically about halfway deep. Run water through leeks to dislodge grit.

Simmer vegetables and green sprigs in spring water, with salt to taste, partially covered, until beets are completely tender and almost falling apart, about 1 hour or so depending on size of beets. Strain broth through 4 layers of dampened cheesecloth, pressing down on vegetables with back of wooden spoon to extract every last drop of goodness.

Bring broth back to a simmer or refrigerate and serve chilled. Just before serving, correct salt and squeeze in lemon juice to taste (I like a generous squeeze of lemon). If serving hot, add lemon juice off heat; the lemon juice itself must not be heated or it will lose its sparkle.

garlic broth/garlic soup supper

The most delectable broth can be made from a head of garlic and a few simple vegetables—carrots, celery, and onions—that are all very much at home in the stockpot.

The vegetables are cut in large pieces and the garlic is left unpeeled. The soup can then be served as a two-course meal—first the broth, then the vegetables and garlic cloves. The sweet, nutty cream is squeezed out of the skins onto thick slices of toasted country bread.

Follow with a small leafy green salad and finish with a cluster of crisp, fragrant grapes and a small handful of unpeeled almonds or walnut halves.

1½ large heads fresh, firm garlic	1–2 tablespoons extra-virgin olive oil
1 medium onion	Freshly grated Parmesan cheese, optional
2 sweet fresh carrots	
3 celery stalks	Thick slices country bread
2–3 whole, unpeeled new potatoes (peeling optional)	
Handful flat-leaf parsley sprigs	
2 quarts spring water	
Fine sea salt and whole black peppercorns	**SERVES 2 TO 3, WITH A CUP OR SO EXTRA BROTH**

Remove papery skin from heads of garlic cloves, but do not peel. Peel onion but leave root end intact. Cut onion in quarters through root end. Peel carrots, if desired, and slice on the diagonal into ½-inch pieces. Cut celery into generous lengths.

In a covered soup pot, gently simmer all vegetables and parsley in water, with salt to taste, and a few peppercorns for 40 minutes to an hour. Stir in olive oil toward end of cooking.

Lift out vegetables and garlic with a large Chinese strainer, and place on a platter. Drizzle with a little raw olive oil and grind coarse pepper over the top. Keep warm.

Ladle broth into bowls. Grate a little Parmesan cheese over the vegetables, if desired, and accompany with toasted or grilled bread.

173.

vegetable soup for children, 1932

This simple soup was created for the tender taste buds of young children. The recipe comes from *The Quality Cook Book,* written by Dorothy Fitzgerald in 1932. It is a wonderful way to introduce to impressionable senses all the living flavors found in nature.

Gimmick-ridden dishes that make food into a form of entertainment rather than a source of pleasure and sustenance, start children off on a very wrong track. Foods from jars and cans have little nutrition to offer, and the drab colors, and dull and lifeless flavors, rob children of any concept or understanding of natural and fresh flavors; they begin life with dulled sensory awareness.

As a baby, I was never fed so-called baby food, nor as a child, was I ever fed anything that was made to look like something else, and for that I'm grateful!

Here's the recipe as it was written in 1932.

4 young carrots	½ bunch parsley
2 potatoes	½ cup rice
Large handful spinach	
3 stalks celery	**SERVES 4**

Wash and dice potatoes, celery, and carrots. Put in boiling water, and cook until tender. Mince the parsley, and clean and mince the spinach, and add to broth. Add rice, and cook until rice is done; add pepper and salt before serving.

into the garden

purslane soup

Maurice Mességué's *C'est la Nature Qui a Raison,* available in English translation, is full of wisdom about the healing powers of herbs, vegetables, and fruits. The book ends with a few recipes that are as connected to the garden as cooking can be. Here's a simple recipe that contains the essence of good cooking.

"Purslane is a common garden weed with high nutritive value and a unique taste. Do not hoe the plants up ruthlessly; save a few for cooking. They are spreading plants with thick leaves and reddish stalks.

"Pick a cupful of the leaves and wash them carefully, for they tend to be gritty. Drop them into a quart of boiling water or meat stock. Add some lettuce leaves or some sorrel, some green beans or peas, some chervil, a chopped onion and a bit of sugar. Let the mixture simmer for a quarter of an hour. At the end, add a dash of fresh cream or a lump of butter and serve the soup with croutons or toasted bread."

spring soup

When the spring sun finally shines on the dark, cool earth of winter, seeds and vines and slender roots feel a quickening within. Miracles begin to happen as the first vegetables take shape and color.

In this soup that celebrates the new season, fine-cut spring vegetables glow like jewels in a sweet pool of creamy new potatoes. If small, sugary fresh peas are not available, do not substitute frozen peas; just add slivers of snow peas or sugar snap peas.

1 pound new potatoes	1 pound unshelled peas, about 1/2 cup shelled
Fine sea salt	Handful small fava beans
1 quart spring water	2 tablespoons unsalted butter
3 garlic shoots, tender white and green portions	Black pepper
1 leek, white base split in half lengthwise	Snipped chives
3 medium carrots, peeled	
1/2 pound skinny asparagus	**SERVES 4**

Peel potatoes and cut into rough dice. Cook potatoes in salted boiling water until tender. Put through finest disk of food mill.

Thinly slice garlic shoots and leek. Cut carrots into small dice and asparagus into very short pieces. Shell peas and peel favas. Sauté all vegetables except fava beans very briefly in butter and a pinch of salt, stirring very gently, until vegetables are just tender.

Bring potato puree to a simmer. Heat milk and stir into soup. Add cooked vegetables with all their juices, and fava beans, and simmer until favas are tender.

To serve, ladle into soup bowls, grind pepper over top, and sprinkle with snipped chives.

found soup

Now that you are in the habit of saving all the vegetable trimmings, dried bread, and other treasures, it is time to make soup.

If, for example, you just served a big platter of Beet Salad with Bright Pepper Topping (see page 125) and saved the fresh, green beet leaves, discard the ribs and stems and cut the leaves into short strips. Simmer in a little salted spring water along with a few pieces of the dried rind of grating cheese cut into small squares. Add a few crushed garlic cloves if desired. After 20 minutes the cheese rind will soften and impart its flavor to the soup.

To serve, place a slice of dried country bread in the bottom of a shallow soup bowl. Drizzle with good olive oil and ladle soup over the top.

If you have it on hand, a tender zucchini cut into small dice would make a lovely addition cooked along with the greens.

autumn supper.

Freshly Harvested Walnuts in the Shell/a Nutcracker

Red Squash and Bread Soup

Bitter Field Salad

Cotognata, Quince "Candy"

red squash and bread soup

Italians call winter squash *zucca rossa*, red squash. The best of the winter squashes do have an orange color so deep it is almost red.

For this sublimely good, utterly simple soup, I use kabocha squash, freshly harvested and straight from a local farm. When cooked, the flesh turns as sweet and dense as pudding.

If you can't find kabocha squash, hubbard or butternut squash make worthy substitutes.

2 1/2 pounds kabocha squash	Fine sea salt
6 cups spring water	4 cups diced, untrimmed country bread
12 garlic cloves, peeled and left whole	Grated Parmesan cheese
4 large fresh sage leaves	**SERVES 6**

Cut squash in half, and scoop out seeds and fibers. Bake at 450°, cut side down, for 30 minutes, or until tender.

Use a teaspoon to scoop out flesh from squash shells and add directly into soup pot. Add water, garlic, sage leaves, and salt. Stir. Bring to a boil, then simmer for 20 minutes, with the lid partially off. Add bread, cover, and let rest, off heat, for 5 minutes. Stir well, then cover for another few minutes.

Ladle soup into serving bowls and generously grate Parmesan cheese over top.

I remember having lunch in a small trattoria in Lecce, in the region of Puglia. It was ten years ago, and the memory is still fresh. It was raining outside, and the city's beautiful baroque buildings worked in limestone were a golden and glowing backdrop to shiny silver streets and dark gray, thundery sky.

The trattoria, a simple place with an adjoining rosticerria, was packed with elegant people, casually dressed. Small lamps glowed in the stormy light, brightening the cloud-darkened interior, making it cavelike and cozy.

Patrons sat in small, barrel-shaped chairs as small as children's chairs, and with big soup spoons contentedly consumed bowls of chick pea and pasta soup. No doubt they had been eating this same soup since childhood and would continue to eat it through old age, always finding in it comfort and reassurance.

eating chick pea soup in Lecce
(LECCE)

mességué's dried pea and fresh tarragon soup

Split-pea soup made in traditional ways can be rather dull and stodgy. Here, it is the fresh, licorice-sweet tarragon and quick cooking that wake up drowsy split-pea soup. The tarragon adds its lilting notes and luminous green color to the soup's muted flavor and appearance.

Always buy dried legumes and beans from a reliable source. If stored too long, they lose flavor and nutrition, and cooking times increase. Look for split peas with a lively green color.

½ pound split peas, about 1⅓ cups	Unsalted butter
4 cups spring water	
Fine sea salt	
1 bunch tarragon, about ¼ cup loosely packed leaves	**SERVES 2 TO 3**

Rinse the peas under cold running water. Place in a soup pot and cover with water. Gently simmer, with lid on, for 25 to 35 minutes, or until tender, adding salt toward end of cooking time.

When tender, add tarragon leaves and stir. Put through a food mill. Gently reheat.

Place a small nut of butter in the bottom of individual soup bowls and immediately ladle in the soup.

Borage

Borage grows wild in Italy and in other parts of the Mediterranean, its small blue flowers dotting the countryside in spring. The tenderest leaves, with their trace of cucumber flavor, are collected and used in cooking. The greens are used in soups, pasta stuffings, and with rice. Earthy lentils and wild borage are a classic rustic Italian pairing.

Borage grows easily in the garden. Like most wild plants, it is vigorous and grows with abandon. The little blossoms not only look lovely, they, too, carry the delicate flavor of cucumber. The blossoms can be strewn over a salad or used as an edible garnish for tea sandwiches, or just admired for the sweet-looking, starry blossoms that are the color of a perfect blue sky.

lentils and greens

The French pair lemony sorrel with their lentils; in Turkey lentils are combined with purslane, also touched with tart lemon flavor. But in Italy it's wild borage that is traditional with lentils. Only the young plants are gathered, since larger leaves are fibrous.

Wild borage is not easy to come by, although its cultivated counterpart can be grown in your garden. More often than not, I make this soup with tender Swiss chard or spinach leaves and include some tomato for a tart, acidic note that brightens the earthy taste of lentils.

½ cup lentils, washed

1½ quarts spring water

Fine sea salt

1 large, ripe tomato, peeled and chopped, or 4 canned tomatoes, without additives, chopped

¼ pound, about 4 cups loosely packed, chopped borage leaves, 1 bunch chopped Swiss chard leaves (without ribs), or 1 bunch chopped stemmed spinach

3 tablespoons extra-virgin olive oil, plus a little for drizzling

Coarsely ground black pepper

4 slices coarse-textured, sturdy bread, preferably a day or two old

Lemon, optional

SERVES 4

Rinse and pick over lentils. Transfer to a soup pot and add water. Simmer briskly for 30 to 35 minutes, or until tender. Season with salt toward end of cooking.

Add tomato, greens, olive oil, and salt. Bring to the boil, then simmer for an additional 10 minutes.

Place a slice of bread in the bottom of 4 soup bowls. Ladle soup over bread, top with a few drops of olive oil and generous freshly ground pepper. Add a few drops of lemon juice, if desired, to sharpen flavors.

big, big soup

I was in the mood for soup in a big way. I decided I would make enough soup to last me a week, but I didn't have a lot of time. What did I do? I filled my biggest soup pot with all the vegetables in my refrigerator, quickly cut into rough dice or coarse slivers. Since the produce was organic, there was no need to peel the carrots or potatoes. My pantry was stocked with canned organic chick peas and canned organic whole peeled tomatoes. Those went into the pot, too. Then I added spring water, filling the pot almost to the brim, and let the soup simmer for about an hour. No sautéing of vegetables, no blanching, no adding vegetables in stages.

I enjoyed it that evening and the following days in a number of ways: first, as a vegetable soup, with gratings of Parmesan or Pecorino Romano cheese; next day, I poached a beautiful piece of halibut in some of the soup to make a quick zuppa di pesce: the third night, I ladled some over a crust of dried bread; during the day, I sipped the broth as a savory tea, and so forth.

1 bunch carrots, tops trimmed, sliced crosswise medium thick

1 whole head celery, including leaves, sliced crosswise medium thick

3 onions, diced medium thick

Handful peeled garlic cloves

Handful mint leaves

1 big slice banana squash, peeled and coarsely diced

1 small green cabbage, cut in half, cored and shredded

4–5 new potatoes, roughly diced

1 Hungarian wax pepper, or other fresh hot pepper to taste, sliced

1 bunch basil, leaves only

1 bunch flat-leaf parsley, leaves and stems coarsely chopped

Two 28-ounce cans organic whole peeled tomatoes

2 cans organic chick peas

Spring water

Fine sea salt and abundant coarsely crushed black pepper

ENOUGH TO FEED A SMALL ARMY

Place all prepared vegetables and herbs in a 12-quart soup pot. And canned peeled tomatoes, crushing them in your hand as you add them to the soup, and all the juices. Add chick peas and juices. Cover generously with water. Season with salt and pepper.

Bring to a boil and let simmer for about 1 hour. As water level drops, keep adding more water so that there is plenty of broth. When soup is almost done, taste for salt and add as needed.

Cooling Soups.

There are very few ice-cold soups that I'm fond of. My favorite is gazpacho and its various permutations.

On the other hand, soups at room temperature or barely chilled can be delicious served on a hot day. For example, in Italy in the summer, minestrone is served at room temperature, with a bit of pesto stirred in at the last moment. Pappa al Pomodoro, tomato and bread soup (see *Cucina Rustica*, page 139), is often served at room temperature.

Here are some of the soups in this chapter that taste wonderful served at room temperature or lightly cooled.

Beet and Lemon Broth (page 172)

Red Squash and Bread Soup (page 179)

Lentils and Greens (page 183)

Big, Big Soup (page 184)

unplugged gazpacho

Gazpacho. We all love it. It provokes our appetites in the heat of summer like no other food. Why do we mistreat it by subjecting it to the awful blades of the processor? Why do we insist upon using abominable canned tomato juice and "pink" supermarket tomatoes when this soup is all about the ripeness of summer—dark red tomatoes bursting with juices, moist cooling cucumbers, sweet red onions?

My version dispenses with all the diced vegetable toppings. It is closer in spirit to the original gazpacho, which predates the tomato, and was simply a dish of sliced cucumber and onions, salted and allowed to rest until the juices formed.

Here, the tomatoes are put through a food mill, the vegetables are cut into thin slivers to promote them to cast their juices into the soup, and garlic, pounded with oregano and cumin, is stirred in.

1 English cucumber, peeled and seeded	2 cups cool spring water
$\frac{1}{2}$ very small red onion	2 tablespoons extra-virgin olive oil
Fine sea salt	2 tablespoons raw red wine vinegar, optional
4 large, juicy red ripe tomatoes, about 2 pounds	$1\frac{1}{2}$ cups rustic bread cubes, $\frac{1}{2}$ inch square
4 garlic cloves, peeled	Ground cayenne pepper
Big pinch each ground cumin and dried Mediterranean oregano	**MAKES 1½ QUARTS**

Slice cucumber into eighths lengthwise. Cut across lengths slightly on the diagonal to create thin slivers. Keeping the root end intact, slice onion lengthwise into quarters, then cut across to make short, thin slivers. You should have about ¾ cup slivered onions. Place cucumber and onion in a shallow serving bowl, add about 1 teaspoon salt, stir and set aside.

Roast tomatoes very briefly over a gas flame just until skin pops and splits in a few places. Cut out core, peel, and gently seed tomatoes without forcing out too much liquid. Coarsely chop half a tomato. Cut remaining tomatoes into chunks and put through the medium-size screen of a food mill. Add tomato puree and chopped tomato to bowl, and stir.

Crush garlic with salt in a mortar and pestle. Add cumin and oregano, and lightly pound. Add to mixture. First stir in water, then olive oil. Add vinegar if tomatoes require a touch of tart flavor for balance. Add salt to taste. Refrigerate.

Meanwhile, sauté bread cubes without oil until they are crisp but not browned. Set aside.

To serve, scatter bread over surface of soup and sprinkle with a little oregano and cayenne.

stews for daily life

189.

stews

Who ever said that a stew must contain a list of ingredients a mile long? My favorite stews usually consist of a few simple ingredients—complementary in flavor and satisfying. Fairly rapid cooking allows the individual flavors and textures to come through along with an intermingling of essences. Stews are quick to put together and they satisfy the appetite in a direct way.

Stews that honor a particular season are put together in a slightly more elaborate style. But while the number of components is greater than usual, the cooking is just as basic. Simply add the ingredients in a staggered fashion so that they arrive at the right point of doneness more or less simultaneously.

As with any cooking, from simple to complex, stews require some respectful attention at the stove to ensure that distinct and intact textures are retained; that is, the ingredients should not all break down and become indistinguishable from one another. I'm not talking precision timing here—a little overcooking or undercooking doesn't matter (I don't mean ingredients that are still somewhat raw, but ones that perhaps haven't had enough time to get acquainted with the rest of the flavors in the pot).

Feel your way toward the timing, since it generally makes no real difference at all if the stew cooks a little more or a little less, it only creates slightly different eating experiences. So just relax and enjoy the process and the results.

the best food in the whole world

Eloquent, simple everyday food is the best food in the world. It doesn't challenge or confuse or attempt to dazzle. In its familiarity it tastes better, is more nurturing, and conveys more meaning than any fancy layered, shaped, and tortured dish that you make once and never make again.

celery stew with almonds

Here, celery finally gets a chance to show off its unique herbal-mineral qualities. Almonds contribute substance and crunch, a surprising and delightful contrast to the soft, tender vegetables.

The outermost celery stalks tend to be spongy and have an overabundance of tough strings. Don't discard them, since they can contribute flavor to a broth. The tender white inner stalks have exquisite flavor and tenderness, best appreciated raw. Select green stalks with full flavor and firm flesh, from the middle portion of the bunch and don't forget to use the fragrant leaves.

1 pound small red potatoes, about 8 or 9

6 large celery stalks, leaves reserved, largest strings removed from stalks

2 cups spring water

2 tablespoons extra-virgin olive oil

Fine sea salt

$\frac{1}{4}$ cup raw, unpeeled almonds

Freshly ground black pepper

SERVES 2 TO 3

Pare away any bruises or blemishes on potatoes. Cut celery into short sections, about 1½ inches long. Coarsely chop celery leaves.

In a medium pot, combine water, olive oil, potatoes, celery and celery leaves, and salt to taste. Bring to a boil, then simmer, partially covered, for 20 minutes, or until vegetables are tender but still hold their shape. Cover and let rest for 5 minutes.

Meanwhile, toast almonds. Spread unpeeled almonds on a baking sheet. Bake at 350° for 12 minutes, or until almonds are highly fragrant. Let cool, then very coarsely chop almonds.

Ladle stew into bowls, and sprinkle with almonds and crushed black pepper. If desired, place a cruet of olive oil on the table for drizzling into the soup.

*The core and leaves of celery are superb
served raw in salads, or cooked in soups,
pasta, or risotto (see Pink Risotto with
Celery, in Verdura, page 232, which features
the stalks, core, and leaves of celery).
For a special treat, I trim the core, which is
solid, juicy, crisp celery meat, and eat it—
sliced, right from my knife to my mouth.*

don't throw it away.

restless America.

Our melting-pot American culture produces a certain restlessness, which often manifests itself in our eating habits. We could probably eat a different culture's cuisine every night for years if we explored all of those represented here in this country.

People in America must believe that Italians eat the most extraordinary range of foods. In fact, each region of Italy is like a separate country, and Italians really do mainly eat the food of their region.

Italians don't tire of dishes they grew up with; it's the familiar foods that they crave—cooked greens, pasta with fresh tomato sauce, fish dressed with lemon juice, simple vegetables that change with the seasons, fresh fruits at the end of the meal.

There is a calm and peace that results from this simple kind of eating. And I believe our bodies are grateful, since the constant assimilation of new tastes and hot spices must be taxing.

I'm not suggesting being a culinary isolationist. I believe there is much to learn and experience from other cultures. However, I feel it would behoove us to slow down a bit and allow these foods to become integrated into our cooking at a slower pace.

Also, it seems impossible and not necessarily desirable to adopt the cooking of another culture in a wholesale manner. Although the eating styles of Mediterranean cultures may be ideal for those who live in the Mediterranean area, they may not be ideal or practical for people in Kansas—different climates, terrains, and traditions are important influences on how people eat.

If you veer too far from your own food traditions, eating won't satisfy you on an emotional level, and the new dish will be a one-time novelty instead of becoming a part of your cooking repertoire.

Make changes gradually, so that new foods can become invested with their own new meanings. Small changes are stepping stones along the way to more profound change.

stewed tomatoes and green pepper

If you've been the victim of the ordinary canned variety, it is time to restore stewed tomatoes to their original luster. Make this dish in late summer only, when tomatoes are gloriously ripe and rampant, peppers are fleshy and deep green, and onions are crisp and juicy.

The ingredients may sound prosaic or predictable, but the flavor isn't. Simple and pure, the stew captures the heart and soul of summer. Serve it with bruschetta, a thick slice of grilled country bread, generously rubbed with fresh garlic.

1 tablespoon extra-virgin olive oil

4 ripe medium tomatoes, peeled, quartered, and seeded

1 onion, peeled, quartered through root end, thickly sliced

Fine sea salt

1 green pepper, cored and seeded, cut into ¼-inch strips

8–9 small basil leaves

SERVES 2 TO 3

Place olive oil in a medium braising pan. Add tomatoes, onion, and salt. Simmer, covered, for 10 minutes. Stir in green pepper, cover, and cook for another 10 minutes. Cool to tepid or room temperature. Stir in whole basil leaves before serving.

eggplant and chick pea stew

Chick peas fortify this rich-tasting stew fragrant with mint and spiked with hot red pepper.

1 pound eggplant, globe or Japanese

Fine sea salt

4 medium onions, diced small

4 tablespoons extra-virgin olive oil

2 garlic cloves, peeled and chopped

1/4 teaspoon dried crushed hot red pepper

1 teaspoon dried whole mint leaves, crushed

5–6 red, ripe medium tomatoes, about 2 pounds, peeled and coarsely diced

2 cups cooked chick peas with 3/4 cup cooking liquid

Coarsely chopped flat-leaf parsley

Lemon wedges

SERVES 4

Peel eggplant and cut into 1-inch dice. Sprinkle lightly with salt and drain in a colander.

In a medium pot, sauté onions in olive oil until golden, about 12 minutes, adding garlic, hot red pepper, and dried mint in the last few minutes of cooking.

Wipe eggplant dry and add to pot. Sauté for 10 minutes over low heat. Add tomatoes, chick peas, and liquid, and cook, covered, for 30 minutes, or until eggplant is meltingly tender but holds its shape. Let rest for 10 minutes. Before serving, sprinkle with fresh parsley.

Serve with lemon wedges.

spring stew

Spring is such an exquisite time of year, with tender blossoms everywhere and the first of the brave little vegetables that have poked their sleepy heads out of the dark earth to smile at the sun.

Make a spring stew, but do it in a spontaneous way. Simply gather whatever vegetables beckon to you, bring them home, give them a bit of a trim (they won't need much because they are young), and set them to cook briefly in a little butter and water.

Unsalted butter	Spring water
A scattering of coriander seeds	Small handful sugary peas
A bit of red onion, diced	A few asparagus stalks
A few morels	Very small handful young fava beans
A carrot	
A few miniature artichokes	Fine sea salt and black pepper
Fine sea salt	**MAKES 2 SMALL SERVINGS**

After some superficial trimming, cut up vegetables into small pieces.

Over low heat, melt a tablespoon or two of butter in a pot and sprinkle in a few coriander seeds. Add red onion and let it give off a bit of its moisture and absorb some of the sweet butter flavor. Add morels and stir a few times.

Now add the sturdy vegetables—the carrot and artichokes—along with a sprinkling of salt. Sauté until tender, adding a few big spoonfuls of water to keep everything very moist. If the peas aren't very tiny, add them at this point, since they'll need a bit more cooking. Keep adding spoonfuls of water to maintain a small amount of broth. Finally, add the very quick-cooking vegetables—tiny peas, asparagus in small dice, and fava beans—adding salt again and a bit more water.

Off the heat, stir in a few scrapings of butter and a generous grinding of pepper. Serve in shallow pasta bowls.

artichokes: the cooked and the raw

I've come to the conclusion that cooking an artichoke whole delivers the richest flavor. When the artichoke is trimmed too closely, its flavor dims. Cooked with leaves, stems, and even the choke, the sweet mineral flavor emerges strongly and clearly.

On a practical level, simply trimming the thorny tops from the leaves takes only a few seconds, as does pulling the choke out of the cooked artichoke.

The stem's flesh is deliciously reminiscent of the heart, so always cook it along with the artichokes.

Very fresh artichokes can be eaten raw. Large ones require being trimmed very closely, then sliced very thinly. Tiny artichokes are so supple that it suffices just to pull off a few of the coarse outer leaves. Or you can simply dip the base of the untrimmed miniature artichoke in olive oil and salt and eat the tender bottom in one bite.

rustic artichokes and potatoes

This dish appeared regularly when I was growing up. I can still see the dinner table, plates piled high with spent artichoke leaves, the vestiges of a meal enjoyed with gusto. I loved it, and that love has not diminished one bit.

I find that the less one trims an artichoke, the stronger the artichoke flavor. Here, only the thorny tops of the leaves are removed so that none of the artichoke's essence is lost.

In this simple presentation, rich, savory artichokes are paired with mellow potatoes, and the juices, incredibly sweet, are soaked up with good bread or drunk straight from the bowl!

If desired, before cooking the artichokes, gently spread open the leaves and spoon in a stuffing of homemade coarse dried bread crumbs and garlic moistened with olive oil. A few small pieces of anchovy can be added to the breadcrumb stuffing.

4 medium artichokes

4 garlic cloves, peeled and coarsely chopped

2 cups spring water

2 tablespoons extra-virgin olive oil

Fine sea salt

1 pound large boiling potatoes

Freshly ground black pepper

SERVES 4

Select a braising pan just large enough to contain vegetables.

Trim about 1 inch from tops of artichoke leaves. With scissors, cut away any remaining thorny tops. Cut off stems so artichokes stand upright. Reserve stems.

Stand artichokes in braising pan and add stems. Sprinkle with garlic. Add water, olive oil, and salt. Peel potatoes and cut into quarters lengthwise. Wedge potato quarters between artichokes.

Cover with a very tight-fitting lid. Cook over medium heat for 25 minutes, or until artichokes and potatoes are tender when pierced with a thin wooden skewer.

continued

Every so often, spoon cooking juices over artichokes (lift lid slowly, directing the steam away from you, so as to prevent being burned). Add water as necessary. There should be enough juices remaining so that each serving can be moistened with 3 to 4 tablespoons of broth.

Sprinkle each artichoke with a little coarse pepper. Each person eats the artichoke leaf by leaf, then removes the choke and eats the heart with fork and knife. Place a bowl on the table for discarded leaves and chokes.

refined artichoke and potato stew

A table strewn with artichoke leaves, as beautiful as it looks, may not always fit your mood or the occasion. The following elegant little stew pairs new potatoes with closely trimmed artichokes, prepared in the Roman style—lavished with slivered mint leaves. Eaten with fork and spoon, with no inedible bits and pieces to intrude upon its succulence, the stew vanishes without leaving a trace.

Serve surrounded with little crostini.

1/2 lemon

4 medium artichokes

3 medium new potatoes, about 3/4 pound

4 tablespoons extra-virgin olive oil

2 large garlic cloves, peeled and finely diced

3 tablespoons chopped flat-leaf parsley leaves

1/2 cup slivered mint leaves

Fine sea salt and black pepper

1 cup spring water

Pecorino Romano cheese, optional (the stew will be less sweet, a little more tangy)

SERVES 4

Use lemon to rub cut portions of artichoke as you work, to avoid discoloration. Snap back and pull down tough outer leaves of artichoke. Slice off tops of remaining leaves, leaving about 1 inch of tender pale yellow leaves. Trim away stem and reserve. Use paring knife to cut away dark green portions on surface of leaf base and stem. Cut artichoke in quarters and cut away choke. Cut stem into short lengths.

Peel potatoes. Cut into medium dice and rinse under cool water.

In a medium braising pan, sauté olive oil and garlic for several minutes over low heat. Add artichokes, potatoes, herbs, and salt to taste. Sauté for a few minutes to lightly coat vegetables with oil. Add water, cover with a tight-fitting lid, and cook at a gentle simmer, stirring occasionally, until vegetables are tender, 20 to 30 minutes. If stew appears to be drying out, add just a little water; too much dilutes the juices.

Ladle into shallow soup bowls, grind pepper over, and drizzle on a few drops of raw olive oil. Sprinkle lightly with cheese for a tangy touch, but only if desired.

dried fava beans with oregano

What we call "rustic food" these days doesn't adequately represent the elemental, earthy quality of real rustic cooking. For a dish to be truly *cucina povera*, literally "poor cooking," it must express both the struggle to survive and the triumph over that pain through a profound and direct sensory experience of the most basic foods.

To savor this dish to its fullest, you must eat the fava beans one by one, squeezing out the soft cream inside into your mouth, then sucking the skins until they are completely empty. The final picture is dark, chalk-brown fava skins, emptied of flesh, lying in small heaps in bowls that have been wiped clean with honest bread.

1 pound dried fava beans, about 2 cups	3 heaping tablespoons dried Mediterranean oregano
8 cups spring water	Fine sea salt and black pepper
6 tablespoons extra-virgin olive oil	
8 cloves garlic, peeled and crushed	**SERVES 4 TO 6**

Place fava beans in a large bowl and add cool water to cover by 2 to 3 inches. Let soak overnight. Drain.

With a small knife, cut away the dark band across one side of each bean.

In a soup pot, combine favas, water, olive oil, garlic, oregano, and salt and coarsely ground pepper. Cook at a simmer for about an hour, or until broth has thickened and is darkly flavored, and beans are meltingly tender inside.

Ladle beans and some broth into bowls, and serve with bread for soaking up juices.

202.

to cook white beans

Although white beans technically do not require presoaking, it is desirable to do so. When cooking them, be sure to keep the heat steady and very low, below a simmer. This allows the beans to swell slowly without bursting. Beans that split during cooking not only release starch, but absorb excess water, compromising their texture. The cooked beans should be whole and creamy, yet slightly resilient.

This recipe makes a generous amount; cooking 1 pound of beans at a time provides you with enough to use in soups, salads, and stews over several days.

1 pound white beans (cannellini, Great Northern, navy, white kidney, and so forth), about 2½ cups

Spring water

Fine sea salt

MAKES ABOUT 5 CUPS BEANS

Pick over beans, discarding any that are broken or discolored. Rinse under cold running water. Place beans in a large bowl and cover generously with water. Soak overnight or for at least 6 hours.

Drain beans and place in a heavy-bottomed pot. Add enough water to cover beans by at least 2 inches. The more water you add, the more broth you will create to use later in soups and other dishes. Very slowly bring water to a bare simmer, then reduce heat to very low. Cook, tightly covered, for 2 to 3 hours, or until beans are just tender. Add salt about three quarters of the way through cooking.

Remove from heat and cool in liquid to complete the cooking.

white beans with intense green herbs

Freshness is the key here: juicy, crunchy, red onion topping, an abundant amount of fresh green herbs, and barely warmed ripe tomatoes. Plump and glossy with olive oil, white beans never had it so good!

3 cups cooked white beans

3 tablespoons extra-virgin olive oil

3 garlic cloves, peeled and finely diced

1/4–1/2 teaspoon hot red pepper flakes

1 teaspoon each chopped fresh thyme, sage, and rosemary

3 tablespoons chopped flat-leaf parsley leaves

4 ripe but firm Roma tomatoes, peeled, seeded, and cut into wedges (out of season, use best-quality canned tomatoes)

Fine sea salt

Spring water, about 1 cup or less

1/2 small red onion, sliced into thin slivers

Basil leaves

Black pepper

Grated Parmesan cheese

SERVES 4 TO 6

Gently rinse beans in cool water and drain well.

Place olive oil, garlic, hot red pepper flakes, and herbs (reserve 1 tablespoon parsley) in a medium braising pan. Sauté over low heat for several minutes. Add tomatoes and salt to taste. Gently toss in oil-herb mixture, briefly warming tomatoes. Gently stir in white beans and add enough water to create a small broth. Cover and cook for a few minutes until everything is heated through.

Ladle beans and juices into shallow soup bowls. Sprinkle with red onion, torn fragments of basil, and remaining 1 tablespoon parsley. Drizzle generously with olive oil and top with a coarse grinding of pepper. Offer grated cheese at the table.

Virgin Vegetables

205.

virgin vegetables

Vegetable cooking is often considered labor-intensive. I don't share this view, since the less you do to vegetables, the greater the reward.

The following recipes feature vegetables in a state of purity—the ultimate way to appreciate fully nature's extraordinary gifts. Each vegetable is given full attention and total respect, chosen in its season, when it has the most to give us and when we can learn the most from it. And cooking vegetables in a direct, unbelabored way makes it possible to have a glowing array of pure goodness on your table almost magically.

Since every season presents a generous selection of vegetables, we are given an ample opportunity to indulge in nature's offerings to the fullest. Why not enjoy vegetables for breakfast? For lunch treat yourself to four or five different seasonal vegetables; then do it again for dinner.

seasonal glory

Every season has its glories. Out of the darkened winter earth come black truffles and gnarled celery root, a forest of wild mushrooms, and masses of sturdy bitter greens.

Seemingly overnight, spring gardens and fields are showered with blossoms. Tender green blades break through the earth's loamy surface. Herbs begin to flower. Delicate mauve buds grace the tips of willow-thin chives, and tarragon and lovage are reborn. Asparagus arrives and so do fresh favas and rusty-pink rhubarb. And a riot of nasturtium blossoms.

In summer, the air is heady with basil. In the blink of an eye, tender zucchini swell with sweet juice. Strong sun brings the first of the season's eagerly awaited tomatoes; fat, ridged, spicy, and sweet corn the color of white butter.

Then mountains of sweet peppers appear in a fall rainbow of colors—chocolate brown, fire-engine red, daffodil yellow, and aubergine. And there is pale blue squash with saffron flesh.

During the year, gardeners bask in the rewards of their labor as they walk through rows of produce and pick those vegetables that are dewy and tender. Through each season, markets offer sweet-smelling produce on proud and magnificent display.

And all this largesse is ours—we need only pluck it from the garden or lovingly select it from overflowing market stands. We are fortunate; we are blessed.

Stina would not have known what a vitamin was, but she supplied them to us in endless variety. Green, she said, was the color of immortality and youth, and the good God had supplied it to us in abundance. From the first courageous dandelion to the last frost-nipped kale, nearly everything that poked up an inquiring green head would soon find its way into one of Stina's copper pots. No sooner had the shoots of my father's hops vines reached a height of five to six inches than they fell victim to that curved and shining blade. She would tie them into small bundles with a long blade of grass, cook them in boiling water with sprigs of parsley, and serve them *au naturel* with a garnish of crumbs browned in butter and a little salt.

Stina (STINA)
Herman Smith, 1942

A remembrance of life on a Michigan farm in the late 1800s as seen through the eyes of a young boy

not knowing your abc's

Don't think you need to know the vitamin and mineral content of everything you eat. I myself do not have an encyclopedic knowledge of the nutrients of each fruit and vegetable. But I do know how fruits and vegetables *should* taste, and this assures me that they possess the full range of goodness they are capable of offering.

Learn how a ripe garden apricot tastes or a freshly harvested hubbard squash or a just-cut artichoke full of juices: This is how you learn to "read" nature.

By eating the freshest possible foods each season offers, including lots of vigorous, purifying greens, and peak seasonal fruits, you will provide yourself with all of nature's gifts.

Trust in what the earth offers, and when and how it offers it.

hidden treasures

Many edible and highly flavorful parts of vegetables are often thrown away with the trimmings. Keep in mind that broccoli leaves, artichoke stems, the core and leaves of celery, the cauliflower core, spinach stems, the core of lettuce, and much more, are all eminently edible.

In fact, many of these hidden treasures are sometimes even more concentrated in flavor than the vegetable itself. Less affluent and more frugal cultures than ours, or those in closer contact to nature and therefore more respectful of it, look on these "throwaways" as prized treats.

Naturally these hidden foods must be subjected to the same scrutiny and high standards of freshness that apply to all foods. Sprinkled throughout this book you will find suggestions for how to cook with fresh vegetable trimmings, leftover bread, and other items that you may not have considered edible or worth the bother. Look for sections titled "Don't throw it away!"

eating asparagus in Rome.

The best way to serve asparagus is the way I saw it done in Rome one balmy spring night. Seated on the terrace of a restaurant in the *centro storico,* the historic heart of the city, were two couples—sleek, bronzed, jeweled, and impeccably groomed in that style so inimitably Roman. This is what they ordered: first asparagus, then vitello tonnato, and then strawberries.

The asparagus came to their table on plain white plates, completely undressed. Small dishes and cruets of olive oil and vinegar arrived. Then each person began the languid, luxurious task of creating a little pool of dressing on the small dish, then, holding the stalks between fingertips, dipping them in, tip first, and eating them all the way down to the stem ends.

what are fresh shell beans?

A fresh shell bean is still something of a mystery to people in certain parts of the country. But there is nothing mysterious about it.

Shell beans are simply any that can be cooked and eaten when fresh, but can also be dried, stored, and cooked at a later time. The list includes cranberry beans, scarlet runner beans, fava and lima beans, and flageolets, to name just a few.

Depending on the variety, fresh shell beans are available and waiting to be enjoyed from April to October.

fresh cranberry beans

Fresh cranberry beans have a rich, nutty-sweet flavor, just like the dried ones. And the skin of both fresh and dried turns a warm earth brown. But the flesh of fresh beans is lighter, less dense, and if beans are very fresh, they cook in a fraction of the time.

I like to eat fresh cranberry beans still warm from cooking, seasoned just with good olive oil and sea salt.

1½ pounds unshelled fresh cranberry beans, or 2 cups shelled beans	Extra-virgin olive oil
	Fine sea salt
Spring water	**SERVES 4**

Place shelled beans in a pot and add water to just cover. Bring to a boil. Cover, and simmer over medium heat for 20 minutes or longer, until beans and skin are tender. Cooking times will vary tremendously according to freshness of beans, anywhere from 20 minutes to an hour or longer.

Lift beans out of broth, and season with olive oil and salt. Reserve bean broth for later use in soups.

"smashed vegetables" and other lessons

There is a theory that when certain vegetables are cooked until quite soft, then smashed, it increases their nutritive value, since vitamins and minerals become easier for the body to absorb.

I grew up eating "smashed broccoli" and "smashed cauliflower"—it was a family tradition. We knew only that these vegetables were delicious. Probably long ago it became understood that vegetables prepared this way could be more fully assimilated by the body; then it became part of the culture.

Insights and hidden knowledge are embedded in the cooking of a country or a region. It is wise to pay close attention to old traditions and learn from them rather than discard them wholesale, even when popular opinion insists that the old ways are less good.

My book *Verdura* contains two "smashed vegetable" recipes. See Pasta with Cauliflower and Sun-dried Tomato Paste (page 212) and Polenta with Broccoli Sauce (page 238).

don't throw it away.

The fresh green leaves on broccoli stems are tender and flavorful. Use them in soups, in pasta sauces, with other greens, or in simple rice dishes (see page 276).

The broccoli stem is utterly delicious; it is succulent and juicy, akin to asparagus. But do not use large and woody stems. Look for tender, young broccoli, strip off the skin of the stem, and cook until just tender.

cauliflower with fresh coriander

If you have written off cauliflower as uninteresting, trust me when I say that it can be absolutely delectable.

Often, cauliflower is sold when it is too large and too old. Age causes the flavor to coarsen and the delicate fine-textured flesh to become unpleasantly watery and soft when cooked.

Buying cauliflower at a good farmer's market or high-quality produce store can make all the difference. Look for small heads that are very white and unblemished, with "flowers" as small as fists. Fresh young cauliflower cooks so rapidly that it remains sweet-tasting, with a tender but intact texture.

In this dish, inspired by Middle Eastern cookery, the extravagant use of coriander contributes a fascinating flavor and aromatic quality that is hard to define but easy to love.

3 very small heads cauliflower, each about ½ pound

3 tablespoons extra-virgin olive oil

½ cup spring water

Fine sea salt

1 big bunch coriander (cilantro), leaves and tender stems chopped, about 1 cup

4 garlic cloves, peeled and crushed

Juice of 1 big lemon

SERVES 4

Trim cauliflower and separate into florets. Sauté in hot olive oil for a few minutes. Add water and salt, and cook until florets are tender. Add coriander and garlic, and sauté a few minutes until coriander turns bright green. Squeeze lemon juice over and stir.

213.

The trimmed core and stems of cauliflower can be eaten, either raw or cooked with the florets.

don't throw it away.

cauliflower gratin m.f.k. fisher

Sometimes the stories told about food can fill one's senses as much as the food itself. M.F.K. Fisher's description of a simple cauliflower gratin she loved to cook, in an improvised kitchen during her early days in France during the 1930s, has stayed with me for many years.

Her tale ends on a melancholy note, with her unsuccessful attempts to recreate the dish in America—the cauliflower were too large, the cheese waxy. But it was the cream that was the main culprit; it was simply not thick enough.

Then one day at the farmer's market, I saw the tiny, fresh cauliflower that she had searched for in vain; I then remembered having spotted a French gruyère at a cheese shop a few days earlier.

After several attempts, and nearly giving up myself, I finally devised a simple method that works beautifully. Instead of cream I use mascarpone and add it at the end, rather than the beginning, of the cooking. Here are the results, as close and as true to her memories as possible.

3 small, very fresh cauliflower, each weighing about ½ pound, or 2 medium cauliflower

Fine sea salt

Unsalted butter

Coarsely ground black pepper

1 cup (2 ounces) freshly grated French Comte gruyère cheese, grated a little less fine than Parmesan cheese

8 ounces, about 1 cup, mascarpone or crème fraîche, softened at room temperature

SERVES 6

Trim greens and central stems from cauliflower. Break cauliflower into large florets. Plunge into abundant boiling water with a pinch of sea salt. Cook, uncovered, for a few minutes, until the cauliflower is tender crisp; don't worry if the water doesn't return to a boil. Drain well in a colander, then spread on tea towels to absorb any excess water. Break or cut into small florets and cut stems into short pieces.

Butter a gratin dish about 9 inches in diameter and 2 inches deep. Transfer cauliflower to gratin dish and season with salt and pepper. Sprinkle gruyère cheese evenly over cauliflower, reserving 2 tablespoons, and top with a few shavings of butter.

Bake at 375° for 15 minutes.

Place gratin under broiler just until cheese turns golden brown, about 2 to 3 minutes. Cauliflower may also turn golden brown in a few places and that is desirable.

Remove gratin from broiler and spoon soft room-temperature mascarpone over entire surface. Sprinkle top evenly with remaining grated gruyère. Briefly heat gratin in a 350° oven just until the mascarpone melts, about 2 minutes. Sprinkle with generous coarsely ground pepper and serve.

VIRGIN VEGETABLES

fresh fava beans with hot red pepper

Many people who adore fresh favas deprive themselves of the pleasure of eating them often because they dread peeling each bean, which many cookbooks direct you to do before cooking.

This recipe and most of my fava bean recipes specifically ask you *not* to peel the beans. It is the slight bitter edge of flavor in the skin that is part of the joy of eating fresh favas.

Leaving the skin on also protects the bean from absorbing too much water in cooking, which diminishes the flavor and causes the bean to fall apart.

Serve with slivers of Pecorino Romano cheese, red wine, and bread for a fresh fava bean feast for 2.

2 cups shelled, unpeeled, tender green fava beans (very large beans with white or yellow skins are too old and overgrown to cook in this way)

Fine sea salt

Spring water

Extra-virgin olive oil

2 medium garlic cloves, peeled and finely diced

Chopped fresh hot red pepper or dried hot red pepper flakes

2 teaspoons chopped flat-leaf parsley

SERVES 2

Cook fava beans in a little salted boiling water until tender, about 10 minutes for very young beans. Drain well.

Drizzle with olive oil and sprinkle with salt, garlic, hot red pepper, and parsley.

flora thoughts

When I go to ethnic restaurants, I invariably order unusual flora, even though servers often try to guide me to tamer flavors. I have a passion for the whole range of flora flavors found in nature—from greens bitter enough to curl your hair to subtle, poetic zucchini blossoms.

At a favorite Salvadoran restaurant, I always order fried palm blossom for dinner. Lovely green pea shoots sautéed in garlic, and gai lan, Chinese broccoli, are my dishes of choice in Chinese restaurants. In Mexican restaurants I love salads made from grilled cactus paddles, and the taste of fresh epazote, a pungent herb akin to oregano.

a bouquet of greens

If your greens are not yellowed but just limp, trim a little off the stem ends. Arrange the greens, like a bouquet of flowers, with the stems immersed in cool, sweet water. Leave for an hour or longer. The greens will drink up the water, perk up, and revive. Rehydrating them helps greens cook evenly, and become tender and velvety.

rustic mushroom and bread skewers

One's first taste of wild mushrooms is usually a revelation, whether it's fresh porcini in Italy or fresh morels in Oregon.

Although true wild mushrooms are starting to appear in markets in America and are being collected in the wild, cultivated shiitake mushrooms are widely available and carry some of the excitement of the wild varieties.

Here, I thread chunks of fleshy shiitake mushrooms and country bread on skewers, and brush them with olive oil and pungent, wildly aromatic herbs. A quick grilling turns the mushrooms and bread golden brown. It doesn't get much better than this!

6 thick-fleshed shiitake mushrooms, about 2 inches in diameter

8 slices country bread, about the same size as mushrooms

3 tablespoons extra-virgin olive oil

2 garlic cloves, peeled and finely diced

1 tablespoon each finely chopped rosemary and sage

Fine sea salt and black pepper

SERVES 2

Completely trim off shiitake stems and discard. Wipe caps clean with a damp tea towel.

Place bread slices in a 250° oven for 10 minutes.

Combine olive oil, garlic, and herbs in a small bowl, and season with salt and coarsely ground pepper.

Lightly brush mushroom and bread slices with olive oil mixture. Generously stuff herbs into the underside of mushrooms caps.

Thread 3 mushrooms and 4 slices bread on each of 2 skewers (see Note), starting and ending each skewer with bread. Brush with any remaining olive oil.

Lightly oil a grill or baking sheet. Grill or broil skewers, turning on all sides, for about 5 minutes, or until golden brown.

Note: Slender metal skewers work well. If using thin wooden skewers, soak them first in water; use 2 skewers, running parallel and spaced apart, to stabilize ingredients so they don't slip and twirl about.

green peas with a lettuce hat

Frozen foods can never convey the delicacy and sweetness of fresh ones and peas are no exception.

When selecting peas, the true test for freshness is if a pea tastes like sugar when you pop it raw into your mouth. If the pod is bright green, moist, and smooth, and you can feel small-sized peas through the shell, the peas will be sweet and tender and will not disappoint.

1–2 tablespoons unsalted butter	2 pounds peas in the pod, shelled, about 2 cups
10 fresh pearl or very small boiling onions with green tops, trimmed and peeled, or white bulbs from a bunch of green onions	Fine sea salt and freshly ground black pepper
	1 small head butter lettuce
2 tablespoons spring water	
1 teaspoon sugar, optional	**SERVES 4**

Melt butter in a small saucepan. Add the onions and cook over low heat for a few minutes. Add the water, sugar, and peas, and season with salt and a touch of pepper. Gently open the head of lettuce without separating the leaves and upend over the peas. Cover with a tight-fitting lid. Cook over gentle heat for about 15 minutes.

219.

roasted sweet and hot peppers

It may be tempting to add herbs, vinegar, lemon juice, or various other seasonings to roasted peppers, but I've purposely left them out in this recipe. Here, I want an absence of other flavorings—a stripping away of distractions—in order to concentrate on the smoky, garlic-infused flavor of the peppers and the contrast between hot and sweet.

Only 1 tablespoon of oil is needed; the peppers give off syrupy juices that, combined with the olive oil, keep the roasted peppers moist and glossy.

1 each red, yellow, and orange bell peppers	Pinch sugar (if peppers are not sweet)
2 pasilla peppers	2 garlic cloves, peeled and thinly sliced
2 jalapeño peppers	
Extra-virgin olive oil	
Fine sea salt	**SERVES 4**

Use tongs to roast peppers over a medium-high gas flame. Roast the sweet peppers for about 6 minutes, the pasilla and jalapeño peppers for 4. Cover peppers with upended bowl for 5 minutes.

Peel peppers with the blunt side of a knife. Cut in half, and remove cores and seeds. Cut sweet peppers into $\frac{1}{2}$-inch strips, hot peppers into $\frac{1}{4}$-inch strips. Toss with 1 tablespoon oil, salt, sugar, and garlic slices. Cover with a bowl or wax paper, and let rest unrefrigerated for at least 1 hour or up to a day. Stir peppers occasionally while they marinate.

If refrigerating peppers, bring to cool room temperature before serving.

new potatoes in sweet wine

Instead of boiling potatoes in water, imagine the possibilities of cooking them in a golden, aromatic liquid.

Asti Spumante is made from the unique muscat grape, defined by its heady, honeyed floral aroma. If you can bear to sacrifice this sparkling golden elixir to the pot, use it as the cooking medium for very small new potatoes. With a sprinkling of fennel seeds and tart lemon rind, the potatoes take on a heavenly flavor and perfume.

The finishing touch—a brief baking in generously buttered parchment paper.

12 small new potatoes, about 1 pound	Fine sea salt
Asti Spumante or other sweet wine	Unsalted butter
1 tablespoon fennel seeds	Parchment paper
A few strips lemon zest, preferably organic	**SERVES 4**

Scrub potatoes clean. Bring Asti Spumante (enough to cover potatoes generously), fennel seeds, and lemon zest to a boil. Salt generously. Add potatoes. Cook, covered, at a simmer until potatoes are just tender when pierced with a thin wooden skewer. Drain, saving strained liquid for another use.

Lavishly butter 2 sheets of parchment paper. Distribute boiled potatoes between sheets of buttered parchment. Seal edges of paper by making small overlapping folds along length and width of paper until well sealed. Place on baking sheet. Bake at 375° for 10 minutes.

To serve, open parchment-paper envelope and roll potatoes in the melted butter. Serve immediately, sprinkled with a little salt.

layered saffron potatoes

The results of this effortless dish, a simple composition of layered vegetables, will thrill you. Potato slices, imbued with the color and musky flavor of golden saffron, intertwine with ribbons of fleshy, sweet red bell pepper and onion. It's all meltingly tender and creamy, but with the surprising crunch of toasted almonds!

4 tablespoons extra-virgin olive oil, preferably Spanish

4 medium onions, about 1 pound, thinly sliced

4 medium new potatoes, about 1 pound, peeled and sliced very thinly

1 red bell pepper, trimmed, seeded, and cut into slivers

Fine sea salt

1 small packet, about $1/8$ teaspoon, powdered Spanish saffron

$1/3$ cup raw almonds, peeled, toasted, and coarsely chopped

SERVES 4

Place olive oil in a medium pot. Layer in onions, potatoes, and red pepper, sprinkling each layer with salt and saffron. Cover tightly and cook over low heat for 15 minutes. Very gently shake pan occasionally to prevent sticking. Sprinkle with almonds and cook another 5 minutes.

mashed potatoes with watercress

Greens, especially those with a trace of bitterness, have tremendous health-giving properties—within most cultures is the cult of eating greens. Here, creamy mild mashed potatoes provide an intriguing contrast to the strong, peppery watercress.

Remember, don't throw away the water in which the watercress cooks. Pour the juices, however small the amount, into a cup and drink it—that's what I do, and it tastes delicious.

1½ pounds small boiling potatoes of about the same size

¼ pound leafy green watercress or other pungent greens, stems trimmed

2 tablespoons butter, softened at room temperature

½ cup milk, warmed

Fine sea salt and black pepper

SERVES 4

Boil potatoes until tender. Drain. Peel when cool enough to handle.

Simmer greens in a little salted water until bright green and tender, a matter of a few minutes. Drain and coarsely chop.

Use a potato masher or fork to mash the potatoes, adding butter and warm milk. Gently reheat. Stir in watercress, and season with salt and coarsely ground black pepper.

baked potato bar

It is hard to surpass the divine pleasure of eating a baked potato straight up—just with sea salt, a coarse grinding of black pepper, and a little sweet butter.

But a naked, split, and furiously steaming baked potato does invite some imaginative wanderings. Here are a few suggestions for toppings that lean toward the Mediterranean.

When preparing potatoes for baking, never, *never* wrap them in aluminum foil—it undermines the potato by trapping steam and turning the flesh dense and clammy instead of light and fluffy.

1 russet potato per person, each about ¹/₂ pound	Coarse sea salt and a peppermill with black peppercorns
Extra-virgin olive oil	Piece of Parmesan cheese and a small hand grater
Fresh herb sprigs in a small water-filled pitcher	Fresh hot red pepper, finely diced, or some crushed dried hot red pepper
Handmade pesto, freshly prepared and in season	Thick lemon wedges
Finely diced garlic	

Rub potatoes lightly with olive oil. Bake at 425° on middle rack of oven for about 1 hour. Halfway through cooking, poke potatoes in a few places with thin wooden skewers to release steam.

Just before potatoes are ready, arrange chosen toppings on table.

Potatoes are ready when a skewer inserted into largest one meets with no resistance.

to wash spinach

For some of us, washing the sink before washing the spinach may be just one step too many—and that lovely bunch of spinach leaves, blushing pink where the stem meets the root—never makes it into the shopping cart.

Instead, invest a few dollars in a white plastic basin large enough to immerse several bunches of spinach or big handfuls of leafy lettuces in abundant water. Reserve the basin for this purpose only, so that it is always clean and at the ready.

225.

spinaci villa amore

If any single food can restore one's health and sanity, this simple spinach dish did it for me. It was early spring and I was traveling in Italy, generously tasting everything it had to offer, when exhaustion set in. My stomach refused to accept any more food—no pasta, no shellfish, no pastries, no matter how tempting!

I headed for Ravello, a small town up in the mountains overlooking the Amalfi coast. There, I recuperated in my small, green-shuttered room with a view of the vast Mediterranean below. I rested quietly, read, and walked in the garden.

And for dinner each night, I ordered spinach, and only spinach. But what spinach it was! Softly mineral, young, and a vivid spring green, freshly picked, barely touched with sweet butter and a hint of Parmesan cheese, piled high on a simple white plate.

$\frac{1}{2}$ pound spinach with small, deep green leaves, stemmed

Fine sea salt

3 thin shavings unsalted butter

Freshly grated Parmesan cheese

SERVES 1

Clean spinach well in three changes of water. Plunge spinach into abundant boiling salted water for 1 to 2 minutes, or until it just wilts. Drain well.

Transfer spinach to a small sauté pan. Top with butter shavings and a sprinkling of cheese. Toss very briefly over low heat, just until butter melts into spinach, adding a little more salt if needed.

don't throw it away.

Always reserve the spinach stems. Cook them with a sprinkling of salt and just the water that clings to them after washing for about 4 minutes, or until tender. Gently press out excess water. Drizzle with olive oil and fresh lemon juice. This is a tasty dish all on its own.

essential spinach

Lemon and salt are the only seasonings in this simple offering—but you won't want to add another thing. This dish truly captures the essence of spinach—with generous amounts of lemon juice to heighten flavor and offer refreshment.

Prewashed spinach is certainly a convenience, but I cannot in good conscience recommend it. The leaves are generally rather large, coarse, and dull, rather than sparklingly fresh and full of life.

2 big bunches spinach, about 1½ to 2 pounds	Juice of 1 big lemon, about 4 tablespoons
Fine sea salt	**SERVES 3 TO 4**

Remove stems from spinach. (Save stems to cook as a separate dish.) Clean spinach leaves in three changes of cool water, either in the sink or a separate basin. Each time, lift spinach out and rinse away dirt that settles to bottom.

Divide spinach into 4 batches. Plunge each batch into abundant boiling salted water for a minute or two, or until it just wilts. Remove each batch of spinach with tongs and drain.

Season spinach with lemon juice and salt.

a field of pumpkins

A pumpkin field on the California coast

one cool and foggy day. Under the low gray skies, bordered by somber cypress and eucalyptus trees, barely visible through the fog, was a large field of blazing orange, stony blue, and peach-pink winter squashes.

Most of all, there were pumpkins, hundreds of them, luminous under the darkening sky—from small, picture-perfect ones to huge convoluted monsters. The Hubbard squash looked like strangely formed gray-blue boulders from another planet; banana squash, large and elongated, were exquisitely colored but seemed as though they were encrusted with barnacles. And there were smooth, tan little butternuts.

I brought home one of each type of squash and cooked them; the flavors and textures were extraordinary. It was from that point onward that I really began to notice and appreciate the whole range of winter squash available to us, and to understand the importance of freshness even in hard-shelled squashes.

Baking is the optimal (and easiest) cooking method for winter squash. The flesh becomes fragrant, creamy, and dense. Frying or roasting thin slices of squash, or grilling small chunks, concentrates the natural sweetness in a similar way.

To me, canned squash has a "dead and gone" taste; frozen squash is watery, the flavor attenuated. Both are best avoided.

red squash with rose water

Baking winter squash fills the house with a provocative sweet and spicy aroma; and then there is the thrill of peeling away the squash's matte smoky-brown skin to reveal its brilliant flesh.

Brown sugar, maple syrup, honey, or other sweeteners often can overwhelm winter squash's natural sweetness.

Here, a splash of sweetly floral rose water points up the natural sugar found in butternut squash, gently amplifying it without obscuring its delicacy.

A little joke: The pine nuts, which add a soft crunch, look just like squash seeds.

1½ pounds butternut squash	2 tablespoons rose water
Fine sea salt	2 tablespoons pine nuts, lightly toasted
1 tablespoon unsalted butter	
1 tablespoon pure cream	**SERVES 2 TO 4**

Place squash on a baking rack. Bake at 375° until very easily pierced with a thin wooden skewer, about 1 hour. When cool enough to handle, peel off skin. Cut squash in half lengthwise and scoop out seeds and dark orange fibers. You should end up with about 1½ cups of squash.

Over medium-low heat, cook squash with a pinch of salt, stirring often, until excess water evaporates, about 15 minutes. In the last few minutes, stir in cream, butter, and rose water. Sprinkle with pine nuts before serving.

summer baked tomatoes with brown sugar

This old-fashioned dish sounds rather odd, but the results are amazingly good. The brown sugar dramatically deepens the flavor of the tomatoes, but does not create an impression of overriding sweetness.

After baking, the tomatoes emerge looking like perfect, deep red, half-globes, but collapse seductively at the touch of a fork.

5 ripe but firm, fleshy medium tomatoes, 1¼ pounds

A gratin dish large enough to contain tomato halves in 1 layer snugly

Fine sea salt and freshly ground black pepper

4 tablespoons dark brown sugar

6 small basil leaves

2 tablespoons unsalted butter, melted

1 cup coarse dried bread cubes, about ¼- to ½-inch dice

SERVES 4

Plunge tomatoes for 10 seconds in boiling water. Cool under running water. Core and peel. Cut in half horizontally. Place tomatoes, cut side down, in gratin dish. Season generously with salt and pepper.

Sprinkle brown sugar evenly over tomatoes. Bury basil leaves in spaces between tomatoes. Melt butter and toss with bread cubes. Sprinkle over and between tomatoes.

Bake tomatoes, uncovered, at 375° for 30 minutes. Serve warm or at room temperature. When serving warm, spoon any remaining juices over tomatoes. At room temperature, the tomatoes and bread will absorb most of the juices.

poached zucchini with mint and garlic

Whole small zucchini, no more than 5 to 6 inches long, have a delicate sweet flavor. The flesh is dense and fine-textured with a complex network of minute seeds.

To preserve these special qualities, I boil zucchini whole and untrimmed for about 3 minutes—since they are uncut, no moisture is absorbed and the zucchini retain their integrity. The flesh cooks to a tantalizing point precisely between crunchy and tender.

If the zucchini is just picked or straight from the farmer's market, even the untrimmed stem ends contain enough sweet juices to cook until tender. Serve the zucchini with their stems still attached for a lovely, natural appearance.

6 small, firm zucchini, about ¾ pound	Black pepper
Fine sea salt	8 mint leaves
1–2 tablespoons extra-virgin olive oil	
3 garlic cloves, peeled and very thinly sliced	SERVES 2 TO 3

Add untrimmed, whole zucchini to abundant salted boiling water. After water returns to a boil, cook zucchini for about 3 minutes. Drain.

Warm olive oil and garlic in a small sauté pan. Cook over low heat until garlic is very tender but not at all browned.

Slice smallest zucchini in half lengthwise or, if they are a little larger, into lengthwise quarters. Arrange zucchini on a serving platter, and drizzle with garlic and olive oil. Season with salt and coarsely ground pepper. Sprinkle with mint leaves. Serve warm or at room temperature.

Pasta per tutti

233.

pasta under attack

These days pasta has turned into a vehicle for a crazy jumble of flavors. The superb taste and texture of pasta seem to play a diminished role, buried as they are under a mountain of different ingredients.

Pasta, a prime source of protein, is the *raison d'être* for preparing pasta dishes. The characteristics of the pasta, its quality, and careful cooking are all paramount.

The sauce should never overpower the pasta; instead, there should be a thoughtful balance between the two.

When eating hard-wheat (dried) pasta, notice its texture, the slight resistance it gives when you bite into it, and the warm flavor of durum wheat. Think about what flavors complement that wheat taste, and what textures accent the pasta when cooked to a perfect al dente.

With fresh fettuccine, experience the tenderness of the ribbons; taste the fresh egg worked into the soft wheat flour; note the porous surface of the pasta and the way it absorbs the sauce; and see how the brilliant orange yolks turn the strands to gold.

In the recipes that follow, I stay true to my philosophy of restraint. With an elegant simplicity of ingredients, flavors can be truly and fully appreciated.

pasta as the main dish

More and more frequently, pasta is the main course for many of us. The same principles of simplicity apply when the pasta is destined for the center of the meal rather than the beginning.

Tossed with a few beans, a grating of cheese, a bit of seafood, or a spoonful of ricotta, pasta will supply you with plenty of nutrition. There is no need to load it down with an overabundance of ingredients.

Pasta is so seductive, so voluptuous, that if you're ravenous, you could easily consume three bowls of it without realizing it. So, to take the edge off appetites I usually begin the meal with freshly toasted almonds, or a few slices of mozzarella drizzled with olive oil and lemon, or paper-thin bresaola slices. And I make a simple salad to serve either before or after the pasta.

End the meal with a bowl of ripened fruit, either all one kind or a mixture of several. A few ice cubes in the bowl looks alluring and keeps the fruit cool and moist without that awful refrigerator chill that is the death of flavor and aroma.

can cheese be grated in a food processor?

The answer is no.

Grating cheese in a food processor reduces the cheese to tiny particles or chunks instead of translucent flakes that melt immediately on contact with hot pasta and other foods.

Often, tasks we tend to relegate to machines can be accomplished more efficiently and with less effort by simple hand tools.

Case in point: A hand-cranked cheese grater, found in Italian markets, is handsome and sturdy. It clamps onto a kitchen counter or table. It grates enormous piles of cheese in minutes, each flake like a feather.

To clean the grater, I simply knock it against a wooden counter to release any trapped cheese flakes. It also works extremely well for grating dried bread and nuts.

The hard rinds left over after grating cheese make a delicious addition to soups. Drop them into the broth as the soup cooks. The rinds become meltingly tender; they impart a creamy quality to the soup as well as sustenance. Add a dried piece of Parmesan or Pecorino Romano to tomato sauce to enrich the flavor.

don't throw it away.

fresh and dried pasta
what to buy, what to avoid

Pasta all'uova, fresh pasta, is made with flour and eggs. And fettuccine is probably the most famous example of fresh pasta. Even when fettuccine dries, it is still considered "fresh." It is never refrigerated but allowed to dry naturally, then stored uncovered, in a cool, dry place.

When you make fettuccine at home, you can control the quality: by using fresh, organic stone-ground flour and free-range eggs; rolling the pasta out to the thinnest setting; and letting the strands dry properly before cooking.

Avoid purchasing packaged fettuccine sold from refrigerated cases. This pasta, which is packed when moist and kept moist under refrigeration, becomes sticky and gummy when cooked. The texture lacks the delicacy and finesse of homemade pasta; the strands are usually too thick. They should be almost translucent.

The very best alternative to making the pasta yourself is to buy de Cecco or Fini fettuccine imported from Italy. But do not select the long, narrow box labeled fettuccine; this pasta is made without egg in the dough, and the strands have a slippery texture that I dislike intensely. This variety of fettuccine lacks the tender, porous quality of a true egg pasta, necessary for the absorption of butter or cream sauces.

Instead, look for the rectangular box with a clear cellophane "window" displaying neat clustered *nests* of fettuccine. This is a wonderful product that closely resembles what you might make at home; I use it often in my own cooking.

Shaped dried pastas, such as penne and spaghetti, are made with hard durum wheat flour and water, and contain no egg. The dough is stiffer than egg dough, and it is more difficult to work by hand. Although at one time many of the shapes, such as orecchiette and long fusilli, were fashioned by hand, nowadays most are shaped by mechanical means.

Unfortunately, quite a few brands of dried pasta on the market are not good. Even many of the imported brands from Italy made with hard wheat flour leave much to be desired. Of all the domestic and imported dried pastas, two brands have come through for me consistently—de Cecco and Barilla, both imported from Italy and widely available. Both pastas cook uniformly and hold up without splitting and tearing. They cook to a perfect al dente texture, and maintain that texture even after being sauced. Most commercial dried pastas go directly from too hard and raw to soft and overcooked, which is exasperating and sabotages all your best efforts to produce fine pasta dishes.

An Island Memory

Many times I've journeyed in my mind to that tiny Italian island where, in the dead of summer, I first tasted a dish called pasta all'insalata.

The *scirocco*, a mean and nasty hot wind, was blowing across the sea. Torpor had set in. I felt as if I were living in slow motion, barely able even to talk. Smoke from smoldering fires carried the strong incense of wild herbs and parched grasses; the creaking sound of insects was almost deafening, madly rhythmical.

The heat rendered me unable to eat. But the proprietor at Le Campanelle saved me with his version of pasta all'insalata —chewy pasta tossed with coarsely chopped raw tomatoes and basil. It was so refreshing and brightly colored, and the flavors were so immediate, that I revived instantly.

Later that night, feeling renewed, I sat on my balcony for hours, listened to the murmuring sea, and gazed into its dark and mysterious softness, thinking of absolutely nothing but the cooling breeze against my skin.

The following recipes see me through the summer—when it's too hot to cook but the produce is much too tantalizing to resist.

These simple cool "salads," with nary a lettuce leaf in sight, tossed with hot pasta create dishes that are meant to be eaten barely warm. The heat of the pasta slightly softens the edges of the raw ingredients, releasing a flow of sweet juices and a whole summer garden of perfume.

my sicilian summer pasta

The idea for this dish came to me one day when I was lost in a reverie about Sicily—its orchards of almond trees that bloom in February, the cool scent of mint growing under precious patches of shade, and its tomatoes that swell miraculously, from parched soil, under violent heat, into sweet, juicy, deep-red jewels.

2–3 fresh garlic cloves, peeled and finely chopped

1 cup mint leaves, slivered

1/2 cup raw, unpeeled almonds, coarsely chopped

4 large, red ripe tomatoes, or 8 small tomatoes, cut into small dice

1/2 cup (or to taste) extra-virgin olive oil

Fine sea salt and black pepper

1 pound spaghettini

SERVES 4 TO 6

Combine all ingredients except pasta in a bowl and stir gently. Add salt and coarsely ground pepper to taste.

Cook pasta in abundant salted boiling water until al dente. Drain very well and toss with raw sauce.

lemons

HOW do I juice lemons? By squeezing them, more often than not, directly over the food I'm seasoning. This is the most free and spontaneous way to use lemons, without any tools and measuring devices.

This may seem too obvious even to state, but I feel it's important to be close to food, feel it in your hand, and smell the residue of sweet oil on your fingers that perfumes your body for hours afterward.

Start by cutting the lemon in half horizontally. With a small knife, pick out any seeds you see. Then just squeeze lemon over salad, vegetables, or fresh mozzarella, picking out any remaining seeds that rise out of the pulp. Continue adding lemon juice, and tasting, until you arrive at a flavor that is pleasing. Forks, wooden reamers, and old-fashioned manual juicers all work well, too.

Lemons vary in size and in the amount of the juice they hold. For our purposes, a good-sized lemon yields about ¼ cup juice. Just be sure to roll the lemon hard against a counter before squeezing, to free up any juices locked into the lemon's translucent structure.

spaghetti with tender parsley and lemon

This simple summer raw sauce is one of my favorites. The pure flavors sparkle and refresh with every lemony, green-flecked, twirled forkful of spaghetti.

Make sure to use tender flat-leafed parsley; it is one of the great herbs of the world. Curly parsley, commonly found in markets here, has a leaf that is too coarse to be used raw with wild abandon.

Serve with thick lemon wedges in each bowl.

1 pound spaghetti	1/2 cup extra-virgin olive oil
Fine sea salt	Juice of 2 lemons
2 bunches flat-leaf parsley, leaves and tender stems coarsely chopped, about 1 cup chopped	Black pepper
1/4 cup slivered mint leaves	**SERVES 4 TO 6**

Cook pasta in abundant salted boiling water. Drain when al dente (see Note).

Toss with herbs, olive oil, lemon juice, salt, and coarsely ground pepper.

Note: This is one of the few pastas that can be made ahead of time and still taste fresh. If planning to serve it later in the day, make sure to undercook the spaghetti; it will continue to cook as it cools and soften as it absorbs juices. Revitalize just before serving with a little fresh lemon juice and olive oil.

sophia's spaghetti al sugo di pomodoro crudo

This is Sophia Loren's recipe for her favorite summer pasta all'insalata. It calls for not-too-ripe tomatoes (Italians love the tart, lemony taste and crisp flesh of underripe tomatoes), lots of green olives, and a 24-hour maceration.

Although picked before fully ripe, the tomatoes should be vine-ripened to the point where they are reddish but streaked with green. Pink supermarket tomatoes, picked prematurely, have absolutely no flavor.

Sophia's final recipe notes stress that the texture of the pasta must be al dente, and that the finished pasta should be abundantly strewn with grated cheese.

2 pounds not-quite-ripe tomatoes, sliced

2 onions, preferably spring onions, finely chopped

Handful green olives, pitted and cut into small pieces

2 tablespoons small capers, preferably packed in salt and rinsed

Fine sea salt and black pepper

Some chopped flat-leaf parsley and a pinch of dried oregano

2 large garlic cloves, peeled and crushed, but left whole

Extra-virgin olive oil

1 pound spaghetti

Imported Parmesan or Pecorino Romano cheese

SERVES 4 TO 6

Combine all ingredients except pasta and cheese in a tureen. Cover ingredients with a topping of olive oil. Let macerate for 24 hours. Before using, remove garlic cloves.

Cook spaghetti in generous boiling salted water until al dente. Drain well and toss with sauce. Sprinkle with a lavish amount of grated cheese.

unplugging your pesto

Food processors and blenders have been around for so long now that most people only know the machine-made variety of pesto.

The smooth, overemulsified mechanized product has a very dense, heavy feel to it, since the pesto is basically reduced to pap.

Handmade pesto has a more interesting texture with a lightness to it. Pesto made with mortar and pestle is richer-tasting, with a stronger herbal flavor than machine-made pesto. Each time you make pesto you'll feel a tremendous satisfaction, a joyfulness as you watch the ingredients turn into a bright green and glossy "sauce." And the time spent with pestle in hand will give you a heightened appreciation when you sit down to enjoy the fragrant tangle of pasta.

With a large mortar and pestle, there is greater control over the ingredients. You have the ability to determine the texture of the finished product; the pesto lightly emulsifies, but the flavors stay true.

The pesto can be served directly from the mortar, spooned over individual pasta bowls, thus reducing exposure to air, which darkens the color and dulls the flavor. Cleanup is easy and there is no waste.

before making unplugged pesto

If you've tried to make pesto with a mortar and pestle, but given up because it was too difficult or time-consuming, the following guidelines will help you achieve your goal with grace and agility, and just a little muscle power.

1.

Use a very large, heavy marble mortar—7 inches in diameter and 4½ inches deep is ideal, but one that is a little smaller will also work. The weight stabilizes the mortar, so as you work you can apply the necessary pressure.

2.

Select a large wooden pestle. The large bulbous base will make your work go faster. Wood is more yielding than marble and doesn't bruise the basil.

3.

Large, coarse sea-salt crystals help break down the basil.

4.

Select the smallest basil leaves you can find. They have a finer texture and are less fibrous so they break down more easily. With larger leaves, always remove the tough rib that runs down the center of the leaf.

5.

Basil leaves should not be exposed to water. It has a negative effect on the fragrance and damages the texture of the leaves. Instead, simply wipe each leaf with a tea towel. If the basil is not organic, very lightly moisten the towel first and let leaves dry thoroughly. This may sound unbearably tedious, but it is well worth the trouble.

6.

Very important: Add only a few herb leaves at a time to the mortar, tearing each leaf into two or three fragments as you add them. Grind each sprinkling of herbs completely before adding more.

7.

Always work low and close to the bottom of the bowl of the mortar. Keep pushing the pesto down to the bottom to form a small mound. This makes the work more efficient and exposes the pesto to less air.

8.

Grind the ingredients by making small circles to break down the ingredients, and put some muscle into it. When a leaf is tough or resistant, gently pound it into a paste, but always work very low to the bowl.

9.

While working, cradle the mortar in your free arm. This helps you put your weight into the pestle and further stabilizes you and the mortar.

10.

Always add a tablespoon or two of hot pasta cooking water to the pesto just before serving, to thin it a little and to warm it.

unplugged pesto

This is how I make pesto. You'll be surprised to learn that there are no pine nuts in it. In my opinion, the sweetness and creamy texture of pine nuts detract from and dull the herbal intensity.

In Liguria, where pesto was born, cooks add a few leaves of parsley, marjoram, and spinach to preserve the basil's green color. Here, I follow their lead, since all-basil pesto turns an unappealing shade of brown when exposed to hot pasta, a color that does not do justice to the vibrant flavor.

2 cups loosely packed (1 cup tightly packed) small basil leaves

1 small, tender spinach leaf, 4 leaves of flat-leaf parsley, and leaves from 1 small sprig of marjoram (if you don't have all 3, include at least 1 and increase the amount)

Small pinch (about $1/2$ teaspoon) coarse sea salt

2 medium garlic cloves, peeled and lightly crushed

$1/3$ cup grated Parmesan cheese

3 tablespoons grated Pecorino Romano cheese

About $1/2$ cup extra-virgin olive oil

1 pound spaghetti or spaghettini

Extra grated cheese for the table, in roughly the same balance as above

SERVES 4 TO 6

246.

Remove any fibrous ribs from basil leaves. Remove spinach rib. Wipe herbs clean with a dry tea towel. If herbs and spinach are not organic, wipe them with a barely dampened towel.

Place sea salt in a large mortar. Add a few leaves, torn into fragments, and 1 clove of the garlic. Start grinding with the pestle, using a circular motion, until everything is reduced to a fine texture. Add a few more leaves, and grind and gently pound until leaves and garlic are reduced. Continue in this way, adding the remaining garlic clove at roughly the midpoint, until all leaves are ground to a fine-textured pesto. As you work, keep scraping the pesto down into the bottom of the bowl to form a mound.

With the pestle, gradually stir in the cheeses. You will have a very dense mixture. Scrape pesto off the pestle and down from the sides of the bowl into the bottom of the mortar.

Pour olive oil into a small pitcher or measuring cup. Add olive oil in a fine stream, stirring it in with the pestle in a circular motion as if you were making mayonnaise. Add more oil only as the stream of oil becomes fully incorporated into the pesto. One-half cup oil makes a very "loose" pesto. You may want to use less oil for a thicker pesto. Taste and add salt as needed. Put a plate over the mortar to seal off air. Place the mortar in the center of the dining table.

Meanwhile, cook spaghetti in abundant salted boiling water until al dente. Add 1 or 2 tablespoons pasta cooking water to the pesto, whisking it in with a fork. Use tongs to lift pasta, dripping wet, into individual shallow pasta bowls. Quickly spoon a little pesto over each bowl and let each person immediately mix it into his or her pasta (if any time elapses the pasta will start to stick together). Place a spoon in the mortar, so diners can help themselves to more pesto according to taste. Serve with grated cheese at the table.

Please don't freeze pesto, since it causes the flavor to change. To preserve pesto at room temperature, do not add the cheese. Top with a $1/2$-inch film of olive oil to block out air and cover tightly. In the past, pesto was preserved this way in earthenware vessels. Pesto can also be refrigerated.

spaghetti with tomato and fresh ginger

Hot, sweet, exquisitely fragrant ginger imparts a provocative and unexpected note to a simple tomato sauce. Just cook the sauce very briefly, to keep the fresh taste of the tomatoes intact. Buy plump, tender ginger; when ginger dries out, it becomes quite fibrous.

Resist the temptation to add grated cheese; the salt conflicts with ginger's subtle sweetness, and muffles its perfume.

2 tablespoons extra-virgin olive oil	Fine sea salt
2 garlic cloves, peeled and finely diced	8 ounces imported dried spaghetti
$1/4$ teaspoon hot red pepper flakes	10 fresh basil leaves, cut into julienne strips
2 tablespoons peeled and finely julienned fresh ginger	Freshly ground black pepper
$1\frac{1}{2}$ cups canned whole tomatoes with juice, imported or organic domestic	**SERVES 2 TO 4**

Place olive oil, garlic, and hot red pepper flakes in a medium sauté pan. Stir over low heat for 2 to 3 minutes. Add ginger and stir for a minute. Add tomatoes and crush with a wooden spoon. Simmer over medium heat for about 10 minutes, adding salt to taste. The sauce is ready when the juices thicken.

Meanwhile, cook spaghetti in abundant salted boiling water until al dente. Drain. Toss spaghetti with tomato sauce and basil. Grind pepper over each serving.

simple pasta

I keep learning

On one of my mother's visits she made a beautiful pasta sauce for dinner. There was very little in the kitchen—just a good can of tomatoes and an onion.

Using my little green knife with serrated edges that I bought in Bologna about ten years ago and have never sharpened, she cut the onion into very tiny, almost infinitesimal dice.

She cooked the onions for a long time in just a little olive oil, stirring often. She kept stirring the onions toward the center of the pot to make a small mound, to trap the steam released in the cooking, which helped them become tender without adding more oil to keep them from burning.

The onions became sweet and rich and creamy, like a puree. A simple thing, but it made all the difference. The pasta was incredibly good.

It reminded me of the subtlety under the surface of simple good food. It doesn't involve lots of fancy ingredients or equipment. It's about knowing how to create heightened flavor from simple ingredients.

two ways to peel tomatoes

Often fresh tomatoes require a preliminary peeling. This is especially necessary when making sauces: The cooking process causes the skin to separate from the tomato flesh, and no amount of cooking can break it down. In making tomato salads, peeling is desirable only if the skins are particularly tough or if the tomatoes have been waxed. The goal is to slip off the skins without cooking the tomatoes, which should emerge as firm as they are when raw.

To peel just a few tomatoes, impale a fork into the stem end and rotate tomato over a gas flame just until the skin pops and you hear a hissing sound. Let cool a little. With a paring knife, cut out the core, which releases the skin; it will slip off easily.

The best way to peel larger quantities of tomatoes is to bring a big pot of water to the boil. Use a Chinese strainer to lower tomatoes carefully into the water. Count 10 seconds, then lift out the tomatoes with the strainer. Immediately immerse them in a bowl of cold water or place under very cold running water, breaking and diffusing the stream of water with your hands to protect the tomatoes from being damaged by the water's impact. Peel with a paring knife as directed above.

spaghetti gianfranco

One of Italy's premier fashion designers calls this his favorite pasta. It's easy to imagine him twirling his fork in his plate of spaghetti in the crowded Milanese ristorante where he dines with the fashion cognoscenti.

Although shallots don't find their way into many Italian dishes, here their delicate flavor creates a subtle variation on fresh tomato sauce. Barely cooked tomato fillets and whole basil leaves end up tasting very much the way they do in nature.

This sauce won't and shouldn't become "sauce-y."

1 pound ripe Roma tomatoes or other fleshy, ripe tomatoes, peeled	1 shallot, very finely chopped
Fine sea salt	10 bright green, springy basil leaves
½ pound spaghetti	Freshly grated Parmesan cheese
2 tablespoons extra-virgin olive oil	**SERVES 2 TO 3**

Cut tomatoes in half and remove seeds. Cut flesh into long strips. Lightly salt tomato fillets and drain in a colander for about 20 minutes.

Cook spaghetti in salted boiling water. While pasta is cooking, make sauce.

In a medium sauté pan, gently warm together olive oil and shallots over low heat. After 1 minute, add tomatoes, salt, and 4 basil leaves. Cook over low heat for 5 minutes.

Drain pasta well. Toss with sauce and remaining whole basil leaves. Serve with grated cheese.

buying fresh favas

Select fava beans with bright green tender pods that contain small to medium-sized beans. You can feel the size of the beans through the cushiony pods.

Shell the beans right before using; otherwise they lose precious moisture, and their remarkable flavor fades.

I prefer to keep the peel on. It has a slightly bitter quality that makes an exciting contrast to the sweet, fresh bean within.

The skin also holds the bean together during cooking, and allows for a longer cooking time, which contributes delectable flavor to the cooking water.

Fresh favas are becoming more available. Farmer's markets carry them, Italian and Middle Eastern produce markets always stock favas when in season, and they even pop up in supermarkets.

onions of springtime

Spring onions are not to be confused with long, slender green onions, also called scallions.

True spring onions are just starting to appear in markets across America. Their lustrous white bulbs, measuring about two inches across, are full of crisp flesh and sweet juices; and the tops sprout green stalks.

These onions are freshly pulled from the soil before being dried and put into storage. Used raw in salads, they are a revelation, with their light, fresh-tasting "bite." They cook quickly due to their high moisture content, and emerge from the pot delightfully tender.

Look for spring onions in farmer's markets and good produce stores.

fava and spring onion pasta

This dish is my personal, ritual welcome to spring. It always puts me in mind of the monumental piles of fresh, tender fava bean pods and new onions that appear in markets in springtime Italy. Their scent, verdant and sharply aromatic, infuses the very air one breathes.

Needless to say, very large favas, with toughened white or yellowish skin, do not belong in this dish.

2 pounds tender fava bean pods, about 2 cups shelled

2 tablespoons extra-virgin olive oil

3 spring onions, peeled, bulbs thinly sliced

1/4 cup chopped mint leaves

1 cup spring water

Fine sea salt

1/2 pound dried short pasta, such as pennette or penne rigate

Crushed black pepper, shavings of Pecorino Romano cheese, extra-virgin olive oil

SERVES 4

Shell fava beans but do not peel. Cover with a kitchen towel.

In a medium sauté pan, combine olive oil and onions. Cook over low heat until tender, about 10 minutes. Add fava beans, mint, water, and salt to taste. Cook over medium-low heat until fava beans are tender. They will turn a silvery gray-green. Add more water if needed so that you have a little flavored broth. Check for salt.

Meanwhile, boil pasta in salted water. Drain when al dente and return to pasta cooking pot. Add fava bean sauce to pasta and toss over low heat for several minutes to allow flavors to come together.

Spoon pasta and juices into individual bowls. Sprinkle with coarsely ground pepper. With a vegetable peeler, shave a little cheese over the top of the pasta. Drizzle with olive oil.

to shell fresh peas

It's easy to shell peas: Use your thumbnail to slit open the inner curve of the pea pod. With your thumb, slide the peas downward out of the pod and into a bowl.

shell peas, live longer

Don't be afraid of the time it takes to shell peas or dread the prospect. Look forward to it as a relaxing meditative pause in your day.

If you come home from work tired and harried, start shelling peas, and after a while you'll feel much calmer—and you won't have to put on the meditation tape to unwind!

If the dish you're preparing is a simple one, such as pasta with fresh peas, you'll actually be relaxed enough to enjoy the meal!

the freshest grated cheese on earth

At home I usually place a chunk of grating cheese and a small, one-sided grater at the table. I grate the cheese over my own dish of pasta. It doesn't get more "freshly grated" than that!

There is little moisture to spare in hard cheeses that have been produced for long storage. So, if Parmesan and Pecorino Romano are grated in advance, they lose whatever moisture they do contain. When exposed to the air, the cheese flakes turn hard and dry in just a few minutes, and do not melt properly on contact with hot pasta.

innocent fettuccine

Appearances can be deceiving. This pasta looks as sweet and innocent as a child, but hidden among the sweet, fresh peas, carrots, and cream are flecks of fiery hot red pepper!

What is the key to a fresh-tasting cream sauce? Start with pure cream containing no stabilizers or other preservatives. True fresh cream has a light texture and sweet taste that is astonishingly good, totally unlike the "greasy" ultrapasteurized product. Heat the cream only briefly before tossing it with the pasta. Cream that has been cooked until all the water content evaporates thickens into a heavy-tasting, cloying sauce, overly rich, and overly sweet. Such sauces are inedible.

2 tablespoons unsalted butter	1 pound young peas, about 1 cup shelled
¼ teaspoon hot red pepper flakes	¼ cup fresh, pure cream
1 small onion, diced fine	8–9 ounces dried egg fettuccine
A little less than ½ pound sweet carrots, about 6 small ones	Grated Parmesan cheese
¾ cup spring water	A few basil leaves
Fine sea salt	SERVES 3 TO 4

Melt butter in a medium sauté pan. Add hot red pepper flakes and onion. Cook over low heat until onion is very tender, about 10 minutes.

Peel and dice carrots. Add carrots, ½ cup water, and salt to pan. Simmer for 5 minutes. Add peas and remaining ¼ cup water. Simmer for another 3 to 5 minutes, or until peas are just tender. Stir in cream and simmer until it thickens a little.

Cook pasta in abundant salted boiling water until tender but not soft. Drain. Toss with sauce and a few tablespoons of grated cheese. Tear basil leaves into fragments and scatter over top. Offer more grated cheese at the table.

pasta with chinese broccoli

Ever since I first tasted Chinese broccoli, or gai lan, it immediately became one of my favorite vegetables. From the highly regarded and well-connected *Brassica* family, Chinese broccoli is an amazing cross between crisp, succulent asparagus and mildly bitter greens.

In a matter of moments, the stalks turn a vivid, electric green and the cooking is complete. The skin is so tender that it does not require peeling; in fact, Chinese broccoli barely requires any trimming at all. So much pleasure, so few demands!

1 pound Chinese broccoli

Fine sea salt

4 tablespoons extra-virgin olive oil

6 garlic cloves, peeled and finely diced

Small pinch hot red pepper flakes

¾–1 pound short pasta, such as penne

SERVES 4

Trim a little off bottom of Chinese broccoli stems. Cut stems into pieces the length of pasta. Cook broccoli in abundant salted boiling water until bright green and crisp, about 4 to 5 minutes (the water may not return to the boil). Lift broccoli out with a large strainer and reserve water.

Place olive oil, garlic, and hot red pepper flakes in a large sauté pan and cook over low heat for several minutes. Add broccoli and salt, and sauté over low heat for a few minutes more.

Meanwhile, cook pasta in reserved broccoli water brought to the boil. Drain when al dente, reserving about ½ cup cooking water.

Place drained pasta in sauté pan with broccoli and toss briefly over low heat until flavors merge. Add a little reserved cooking water to pasta to extend flavors and keep pasta moist.

spaghettini fioriti

This lovely "flowered" pasta highlights the delicate taste of very young zucchini still sporting their showy saffron blossoms. Very light cooking, sweet accents of red onion, and the slight creaminess of ricotta enhance the subtle flavor of the tiny zucchini and the delicate little flowers.

1 tablespoon unsalted butter

2 tablespoons extra-virgin olive oil

1/2 medium red onion, finely diced

2 garlic cloves, peeled and lightly crushed

1/2 pound tiny zucchini, with very fresh-looking blossoms attached

1/4 cup spring water

Fine sea salt

1/4 cup ricotta

1/2 pound imported spaghettini

Grated Parmesan or a little Pecorino Romano cheese

Black pepper

A few basil leaves

SERVES 2 TO 3

In a sauté pan, melt together butter and olive oil. Add red onion and garlic, and sauté over low heat.

Cut zucchini into medium-thick rounds and blossoms into quarters lengthwise. When onion is translucent, add zucchini and blossoms to pan and gently stir for several minutes to absorb flavors.

Add water and a bit of salt, cover, and continue to cook another few minutes until the zucchini and flowers are just tender. Taste and add salt as needed. Off heat, stir in ricotta.

Meanwhile, cook spaghettini in abundant boiling salted water until al dente. Reserve about 1/2 cup pasta water, then drain.

Toss with sauce, and if dish seems dry, add a little of the pasta water to "loosen up" the sauce. Sprinkle with a few tablespoons of grated cheese and freshly grated pepper. Tear basil leaves into fragments and scatter over the top.

cooking with heat

Cooking should be an active, lively affair with hissing and bubbling pots, and sauté pans emitting sizzling sounds that command your attention.

When recipes call for a broth to simmer or onions to be slowly sautéed, *always* start at high heat and adjust downward to give the cooking process a jump start. This gives you better control, and gets the cooking off to a brisk start.

When making soup first bring it to a boil, then reduce the heat to the correct level. Sautéing onions? Naturally you don't want them to burn, but you do want them to turn golden. Start with high heat for a few minutes, then adjust the flame to a more moderate level.

Starting with heat at a low, cautious temperature causes your attention to drift and your focus to blur. It takes some of the immediacy out of cooking and, with it, some of the excitement.

pasta with onions and crystallized ginger

On a summer trip to Rome, I visited friends who were working on a film being shot at a small movie studio on the dusty outskirts of the city.

One evening at my friends' apartment overlooking the city, they served pasta with a seductive sauce of tender, golden onions spiked with ginger. The heat and scent of the ginger and the onion's sweetness seemed to be at one with the sweeping view of Rome at sunset: a warm, glowing expanse of clay rooftops against a peach and orange-streaked sky, softly on fire from the rays of the setting sun.

3 medium onions	1 pound imported pasta, such as spaghetti, spaghettini, or penne
2 tablespoons unsalted butter	
2 tablespoons extra-virgin olive oil	Slivered green onions
Fine sea salt	
2–3 tablespoons very finely julienned crystallized ginger	**SERVES 4 TO 6**

Cut onions in half through root ends. Peel and slice crosswise medium thin.

Warm butter and olive oil in a large sauté pan. Add onions and salt, and stir. Cook over medium-low heat, stirring often. Lower heat if necessary. When onions are lightly golden and very tender, add ginger. Lower heat and cook an additional few minutes.

Meanwhile, cook pasta in abundant salted boiling water. Drain when al dente, reserving a cup of pasta water. Transfer pasta to sauté pan containing sauce. Toss over low heat for a few minutes, adding water as needed if pasta appears dry. Taste for salt.

Serve garnished with a scattering of green onions. No cheese, please.

fettuccine with mascarpone and spinach

Special-occasion food doesn't need to be pummeled and primped and formed into a pyramid. Nor does it require being enriched beyond human tolerance.

When you crave the pleasures of butter and cream, or when the occasion seems to call for it, golden fettuccine entwined with ribbons of spinach and delicately cloaked in magnificent mascarpone—creamy and light on the tongue, since it is simply warmed through, not cooked—makes a fitting dish.

Infused with the warm spice glow of nutmeg, the pasta is just luscious enough but not overwhelmingly rich.

1 bunch tender, small-leafed green spinach, about 3/4 pound

Fine sea salt

2 tablespoons unsalted butter

8–9 ounces imported dried egg fettuccine

8 ounces mascarpone

1/2 cup grated Parmesan cheese

1/2 teaspoon grated fresh nutmeg

Black pepper

MAKES 4 SMALL SERVINGS

Wash spinach well in several changes of water, breaking off all stems. Drain. Stack leaves and cut into thin strips.

Place spinach in a large sauté pan and cook over medium heat with water that clings to leaves and a sprinkling of salt. When spinach is just barely wilted, tilt pan to drain water.

Return to stove and, over low heat, evaporate excess moisture. Add butter to pan and stir just until it is absorbed by spinach.

Meanwhile, cook fettuccine in abundant salted boiling water. Reserve about 1/2 cup cooking water. Drain pasta when just tender, leaving the strands dripping wet. Transfer fettuccine to sauté pan containing spinach.

Working efficiently and quickly, over low heat, toss fettuccine with spinach. Add mascarpone and gently toss to coat strands. Add half the grated cheese, sprinkle with nutmeg, and toss. Add remaining cheese, a grinding or two of pepper, and toss briefly. If pasta appears dry, add enough reserved cooking water to moisten the strands. Serve immediately in warm shallow pasta bowls.

la formaggiera

A small bowl with a hinged lid specifically designed to hold grated cheese, the *formaggiera* is a common sight in Italian households. In fact, it is a necessary accompaniment to most Italian meals.

The beauty of the *formaggiera* is that half of the lid flips up and down. When closed, it protects the cheese from drying out, but flips open easily when spooning out cheese. Parmesan cheese, once grated, cannot afford exposure to air—it dries out almost instantly. So, this little contraption is integral to Italian life at the table.

Some *formaggiere* are made of stainless steel and glass, very simple and functional in design. Others, crafted of silver and crystal, and finely worked, are treasured family heirlooms.

I have a small collection of *formaggiere*—mostly everyday designs I've picked up in kitchenware shops in Italy. I find them quite beautiful in their own right.

Always save some of the pasta cooking water before draining cooked pasta. It contains flavor and nutrition. The water is used to *allungare*, literally "lengthen," or stretch a pasta sauce (nontomato sauces only) so that the flavor extends to the end of each strand.

For example, adding spoonfuls of hot pasta water to fresh ricotta thins it to a creamy sauce; or a small amount of hot pasta water can be used to dilute pesto so that it, too, can cover the entire pasta strand without the addition of excess oil.

Don't throw away the pasta water.

pasta with potatoes and saffron

Here, potatoes, humble and earthbound, metamorphose into a surprisingly elegant sauce for fettuccine. The secret is to add enough pasta cooking water to the saffron-tinted potatoes to turn the "sauce" lightly creamy, just thick enough to barely cloak garlands of fettuccine.

1 packet, about ⅛ teaspoon, powdered Spanish saffron

1 cup spring water

½ medium red onion, finely diced

4 tablespoons extra-virgin olive oil

3 medium boiling potatoes, peeled and cut into ¼-inch dice

½ cup chopped flat-leaf parsley

Fine sea salt and freshly ground black pepper

8 ounces dried imported egg fettuccine

½ cup freshly grated Pecorino Romano cheese

Handful fresh small basil leaves

SERVES 3 TO 4

Sprinkle saffron into water. Set aside.

Sauté red onion in olive oil for about 10 minutes, or until onion is tender and lightly golden. Add potatoes, parsley, and salt and pepper. Toss potatoes in oil over gentle heat. After a few minutes, add saffron water and stir. Cover and cook for 10 minutes, or until potatoes are meltingly tender.

Meanwhile, cook fettuccine in abundant salted boiling water until tender. Reserve about 2 cups pasta cooking water. Drain pasta. Toss with sauce and grated cheese, adding just enough pasta water for the sauce to cloak the fettuccine lightly. (Too little water causes the pasta to be sticky and clump up.) If desired, drizzle a little fresh olive oil into the pasta when tossing. Sprinkle with basil leaves and serve with extra cheese at the table.

fettuccine with shell beans and dried tomatoes

In summer make this dish with fresh cranberry beans (cooking times vary considerably according to freshness) and sprinkle pasta with coarsely chopped basil leaves. In cold seasons slow-cook presoaked dried cranberry, borlotti, or other red-hued beans, and add some finely chopped sage and rosemary to the onions as they cook.

Egg-enriched fettuccine adds a delicate note to the dish. I really enjoy the flavor and tenderness of fettuccine in contrast with the beans, but dried pasta shapes are equally delicious.

4 tablespoons extra-virgin olive oil

1 small onion, diced small

8 sun-dried tomatoes, packed in oil or plumped in warm water, drained and coarsely chopped

2 garlic cloves, peeled and finely diced

1/2 teaspoon hot red pepper flakes

2 cups cooked shell beans, fresh or dried

4 tablespoons chopped flat-leaf parsley

Fine sea salt

Spring water

8–9 ounces dried fresh pasta

Grated Parmesan cheese

SERVES 4 TO 6

Warm olive oil in a medium sauté pan. Add onion and sun-dried tomatoes, and cook over medium-low heat until onion is tender, about 10 minutes. Add garlic and hot red pepper flakes during last few minutes of cooking.

Gently stir in beans, parsley, and salt to taste. Gently heat, adding 1/4 cup spring water. Cook until beans are hot and herbs are bright green, adding a bit more water if needed.

Meanwhile, cook pasta in abundant salted boiling water until tender but firm. Drain, reserving 1/2 cup pasta water, and toss with sauce. Add reserved cooking water if dish seems dry, a little at a time.

Serve with grated cheese at the table.

A stuffed pasta and a baked pasta.

persian ravioli

Preparing this dish is a heady experience. Masses of herbs and greens, as beautiful and soft to the gaze as a meadow, are finely chopped, to form an intensely perfumed green mountain that becomes the filling for remarkable ravioli.

Traditionally served on March 20, the ancient Persian New Year's Day, the ravioli are a ritual celebration of spring's arrival. The original recipe calls for wild greens—wild spinach, wild clover, shepherd's purse, and so forth. If you have access to wild greens, by all means use them.

The redoubtable Charles Perry discovered this recipe on a calendar being sold on the streets of Tashkent, and translated it from the Uzbek language.

6 tablespoons unsalted butter

1 onion, finely diced

1 bunch green onions, thinly sliced

1 large bunch each very tender new spinach, coriander, mint, and sorrel (if sorrel is unavailable, add a bit of grated lemon peel), leaves and tender stems finely chopped, about 1 pound total

Fine sea salt

1/2 teaspoon, or to taste, ground hot red pepper

FOR THE PASTA
2 cups unbleached all-purpose flour

3 eggs

FOR THE SAUCE

Warm unsalted butter

Ground hot red pepper

SERVES 6 TO 8

Melt butter in a large sauté pan. Add onion and cook until tender. Add green onions and chopped greens, salt to taste, and hot red pepper. Cook until the leaves are wilted and tender.

Remove greens with a slotted spoon and transfer to a bowl. Cook down remaining juices until lightly syrupy and pour into bowl.

Combine flour and eggs, and form into a dough. Knead well for 10 minutes. Form into a ball, wrap in wax paper, and let rest for 30 minutes.

Divide ball into quarters. Roll out a quarter of the dough at a time using hand-cranked pasta machine.

Keep remaining dough covered. Roll dough to the thinnest setting. Cut pasta sheet into 3 × 3-inch squares.

Place a small mound of greens in the center of each square. Lightly moisten edges of pasta with water. Fold over to create a triangle and pinch ends together, then fold opposite points of triangle over each other and pinch together.

Cook pasta triangles in salted boiling water for 3 to 4 minutes. Lift out with a slotted spoon or Chinese strainer. Briefly place spoon or strainer with ravioli on folded tea towel to absorb excess water.

Arrange ravioli on serving dishes, drizzle with a little melted butter, and sprinkle with hot red pepper to taste.

penne baked with sliced tomatoes

A pasta this easy to assemble, that tastes this good, deserves a medal.

½ pound penne	1 tablespoon unsalted butter
Fine sea salt	A small handful of basil leaves
2 tablespoons extra-virgin olive oil	A fistful of grated Parmesan cheese
1 pound ripe, red tomatoes, sliced	
Freshly ground black pepper	SERVES 2 TO 3

Cook penne in abundant salted boiling water until a bit more al dente than usual, about 8 to 10 minutes. Drain well and place in a large, oiled baking dish. Toss with 1 tablespoon olive oil and salt. Top with tomato slices, adding salt and pepper to each layer and flavoring with remaining olive oil and shavings of butter.

Cook at 400° for about 20 minutes, or until the tomatoes start to break down a little. They should still maintain their shape.

Remove pasta from oven and immediately sprinkle with basil leaves, roughly torn, and Parmesan cheese. In the baking dish, toss together tomatoes, pasta, and correct seasonings. Serve immediately or at warm room temperature.

Hot rice/

cool salad,

risotto,

riso asti

MILANO
MARCHIO DEPOSITATO

ITA *Superfino Arborio*
"Enriched" Rice
PRODUCT OF ITALY
NET WT.: 16 oz. (1 LB)
Packed by:
NIBBIO s.r.l.
MILANO-ITALY

and rice dishes

269.

hot rice with cold lemon

Nothing could be simpler than this little dish of fragrant, chewy Arborio rice doused with a squeeze of lemon and a splash of good olive oil.

⅓ cup Arborio rice	Fine sea salt
1 tablespoon extra-virgin olive oil	Freshly ground pepper
1 tablespoon lemon juice	**SERVES 1**

Boil rice in abundant salted water until al dente, about 12 minutes. Drain and transfer to a shallow pasta bowl. Anoint with olive oil, freshly squeezed lemon juice, and salt. Toss for just a moment or two. Grind pepper over the top and serve.

Hot rice / cool salad

hot rice with tomato and mozzarella salad

Hot pasta tossed with tomato and mozzarella has become a standard. But it occurred to me one day that rice would make an equally delicious complement. The heat from the rice gently warms the salad, just enough to release fragrance and melt the mozzarella.

Now I can't decide which I like best!

4 large red, ripe tomatoes, cut into $\frac{1}{2}$-inch dice

Handful basil leaves, coarsely chopped or torn

2 garlic cloves, peeled and finely diced

Fine sea salt and freshly ground black pepper

Extra-virgin olive oil to cover

2 cups Arborio rice

$\frac{3}{4}$ pound fresh mozzarella, shredded on the large holes of a four-sided grater

SERVES 4

In a small bowl, mix together tomatoes, basil, and garlic, and season with salt and pepper. Add enough olive oil to barely cover the tomatoes. Cover with a plate and marinate at room temperature for 1 hour.

Just before serving, boil rice in abundant salted water until al dente, about 12 minutes. Drain and immediately transfer to a serving bowl. Add tomato mixture, mozzarella, and salt to taste. Toss until mozzarella just begins to melt. Serve right away.

green tomato risotto

Fried green tomatoes, pickled green tomatoes, green tomato pie were all part of our cooking traditions when America was chiefly an agricultural country. However, finding green tomatoes these days isn't that easy.

It wasn't until I was writing *Verdura* that I encountered plump green tomatoes and made them into a sauce with basil and almonds for pasta. One taste was all it took—I was madly in love.

Here, the rice becomes completely infused with the taste of green tomatoes. The result is lemony-tart and refreshing, creamy and subtle all at once. Most of the tomatoes "melt" into the muted green risotto, but a few luscious, fragments remain.

Here, too, almonds and perfumed basil add their softly sweet notes to the tangy risotto. Why tamper with perfection?

3 tablespoons extra-virgin olive oil

1/2 small onion, very finely diced

3 tablespoons chopped flat-leaf parsley

2 finely chopped peeled garlic cloves

1 1/2 pounds green tomatoes, cored and thinly sliced

Fine sea salt

1 1/2 cups Arborio rice or other short-grained rice

5 cups simmering lightly salted spring water

1/2 tablespoon unsalted butter

3/4 cup raw almonds, peeled or unpeeled, finely chopped

10 big basil leaves, torn into fragments

SERVES 3 TO 4

In a medium, heavy-bottomed soup pot, sauté olive oil, onion, and parsley over medium-low heat until onions are tender, about 12 minutes. Add garlic in last few minutes of cooking. Add green tomatoes and salt, and stir well. Cook until tomatoes start to break apart, about 10 minutes.

Add rice and stir for several minutes to coat rice. Begin adding water by the ladleful, stirring often until each ladleful has been almost fully absorbed. Then add the next ladleful, and so forth. Risotto is done when rice is soupy but nicely al dente—not too hard at the center, but with a little bite—about 16 minutes. Stir in butter, cover, and let rest a few minutes. Stir in $1/3$ of the almonds and all the basil. Serve risotto in shallow pasta bowls and offer the rest of the almonds in a bowl or *formaggiera* with a small spoon.

wooden spoons

The wooden spoons I recommend are actually flat ones, shaped something like a spatula. Spoons with a wooden bowl at the end actually hinder you in cooking. A flat wooden spoon is just right for sautéing vegetables, a must for stirring risotto and polenta, and works well for tossing salad and for blending ingredients.

The angular shape allows you to get into the corners and along the bottoms of pots and pans. And since the spoon has flat surfaces, food does not get caught as it would in the hollow of a bowllike wooden spoon.

red wine risotto

Rich red wine—dark, profoundly scented, complex, its flavor deep as a well—generously flavors this very special but simple risotto.

1 each small onion, small carrot, and celery stalk with leaves, finely chopped together

A few basil leaves and flat-leaf parsley sprigs, finely chopped

4 tablespoons unsalted butter

1 cup Barbera or other rich, full-flavored red wine

2 tablespoons imported tomato paste

6 cups simmering salted spring water

2 cups Arborio rice

1/2 cup grated Parmesan cheese, plus more for the table

SERVES 6

In a medium, heavy-bottomed soup pot, sauté vegetables and herbs in butter over medium-low heat until tender, about 12 minutes. Add 3/4 cup red wine and cook until absorbed. Add tomato paste and 1 ladleful simmering water. Stir well and cook down for several minutes until water evaporates.

Add rice and stir to coat grains. Continue adding simmering water, 1 ladleful at a time, stirring often. Keep pot covered between stirs. Toward end of cooking, add remaining wine.

When rice is al dente and risotto is creamy and moist, about 16 minutes, turn off heat. Stir in half the cheese, taste for salt, then stir in additional cheese as needed. Cover and let rest briefly before serving.

rich lemon rice

Adding egg yolks to hot rice cloaks each grain in a lightly creamy sauce, as in carbonara sauce for pasta. Tart lemon juice and cayenne pepper temper the richness and imbue the rice with fragrance and heat. If you are concerned about eating raw eggs, rest assured; the egg cooks completely when warmed over low heat.

Garnish each serving with a lemon wedge and pour a crisp white wine or fizzy Prosecco. Follow with a simple, clean-tasting salad of tender greens and herbs.

1½ cups Arborio rice

Fine sea salt

Spring water

3 egg yolks, lightly beaten, or 2 whole eggs, lightly beaten

2 tablespoons lemon juice

⅛ to ¼ teaspoon ground cayenne pepper

¾ cup grated imported Parmesan cheese

2 tablespoons unsalted butter, softened at room temperature

SERVES 3 TO 4

Boil rice in a generous amount of salted boiling water. When rice is al dente, after about 12 minutes, reserve 2 cups cooking liquid and drain rice. Place rice in a large sauté pan.

Add 1½ cups reserved liquid to rice. Stir egg yolks into remaining ½ cup water. Stir in lemon juice and cayenne, and pour over rice. Add the cheese and butter. Gently stir over low heat until liquid slightly thickens. Taste and add salt as needed.

Serve rice in warm, shallow pasta bowls and offer additional grated cheese at the table.

rice dishes

HOT RICE/COOL SALAD...

rice with found broccoli leaves

Broccoli leaves, found along the stalk, are tender, delicious, and health-giving. In this country we throw them away without a second thought. In Italy they are gathered up for cooking.

Broccoli leaves are the province of homely cooking, homely in the best and truest sense of the word: simple and unpretentious and everyday. Recipes like this one usually never make it to the printed page, nor are they served in restaurants. They are traditionally passed along from mother to daughter, and served in the bosom of one's family.

When I make this dish, I ask my friend at the organic produce market where I shop if I can collect all the little leaves he removes from the stalks before putting the broccoli out for sale. He's happy to let me do so since he, too, has a secret passion for broccoli leaves.

2 garlic cloves, peeled and finely chopped

2–3 tablespoons extra-virgin olive oil

6 ounces broccoli leaves, stripped of coarse stems, about 3 cups chopped

Fine sea salt

3 cups spring water

½ cup rice, preferably Arborio

SERVES 2 TO 3

In a medium soup pot, sauté garlic in olive oil over low heat for several minutes. Add broccoli leaves and sea salt to taste. Stir until leaves are bright green, glossy, and a bit wilted, 4 to 5 minutes.

Add water and bring to a boil. Add rice and cook at a steady simmer until rice is al dente and greens are tender, adding salt as needed. The dish should be lightly brothy, a cross between risotto and soup.

three polenta  dishes.

277.

polenta made easy

The only way to get full flavor and nutrition from cooked polenta is to start with unrefined organic stone-ground cornmeal. Do not use degerminated cornmeal, the kind sold in supermarkets; it is just a shadow of its former self.

Here, instead of adding polenta grain by grain to simmering water, you stir together all the cornmeal and half the liquid, and add it slowly to the remaining water, which is boiling hot. This completely eliminates any problems with lumps forming. Although the ratio of cornmeal to water varies with each cook, I find that 1 cup cornmeal to 5 cups water allows for a slow cooking, with only occasional stirring.

The result: a full-flavored, creamy polenta that tastes exquisite just as it is, straight out of the pot.

5 cups spring water	1 teaspoon fine sea salt
1 cup medium-textured, stone-ground cornmeal	**SERVES 3 TO 4**

In a heavy saucepan, heat to boiling 2½ cups water. In a large measuring cup or small pitcher, whisk together cornmeal and remaining water. Continue whisking cornmeal and water as you slowly pour it into the boiling water. Add salt and whisk polenta until it returns to the boil and starts to thicken a bit, about 5 minutes. Lower the heat. Cook at a steady simmer.

Whisk occasionally for the first 40 minutes, then more often during the next 10 minutes. During the final 10 minutes, stir continuously until the polenta mounds on the whisk but is still moist and pourable. Total cooking time is 60 to 65 minutes.

Use immediately or pour into either a moistened gratin dish or loaf pan, depending on use, and let cool completely.

grilled polenta with tomato-mint salad

Going from cool to hot temperatures in a single dish keeps one's taste buds alert and lively, and the results are quite refreshing. And there is that sensual interplay of temperatures, each subtly merging with and enhancing the other.

When polenta slices are hot off the grill, bright gold and a bit blackened and blistered, that is the moment to spoon the salad on top and breathe in the cool, sweet mint and pungent tomato-spice scents.

6 large, ripe but firm Roma tomatoes, about 1 pound

2 tablespoons extra-virgin olive oil

Fine sea salt

$1/2$ cup tightly packed mint leaves

1 medium garlic clove, peeled

8 slices polenta, each about $1/2$ inch thick

Freshly grated Pecorino Romano, optional

SERVES 2 TO 4

Plunge tomatoes in boiling water for 10 seconds. Lift out with large strainer. Place in a bowl and cool under cold running water. Core and peel. Dice tomatoes and place in a bowl. Add olive oil and salt to taste. Stir gently.

Sliver mint leaves and finely chop garlic. Place in a mortar and add salt. With pestle, grind ingredients into a coarse paste.

Lightly brush polenta slices with olive oil. Grill or broil 4 to 5 minutes on each side, or until surface is crusty and marked by the grill.

Stir mint-garlic pesto into diced tomatoes. Arrange grilled polenta on individual plates, and spoon tomatoes and juices over the top. If desired, sprinkle with grated cheese.

polenta "custard" with summer vegetable stew

Polenta is not only cooked in water, sometimes it is cooked in milk. This results in a creamy polenta that has a custardlike quality both in taste and texture.

Here, a mound of steaming polenta "custard" is surrounded with a quick, colorful, and abundant summer stew. The dish is easily put together and quite beautiful.

FOR THE POLENTA

2½ cups spring water

2½ cups lean or leanest milk

1 cup fine-textured stone-ground cornmeal

Fine sea salt

FOR THE STEW

6 ounces small green beans, trimmed

Fine sea salt

2 tablespoons extra-virgin olive oil

1 bunch green onions, root ends trimmed and a few inches cut off the tops, cut into short lengths

2 yellow bell peppers, cored, seeded, and cut into ½-inch squares

1 basket small pear or cherry tomatoes, all red, or a mix of red, yellow, green, and gold

¾ cup grated Parmesan or Pecorino Romano cheese

Coarsely ground black pepper and a small handful basil leaves

SERVES 4

To make the polenta, bring water to a boil in a heavy saucepan. In a large measuring cup or small pitcher, whisk together milk and cornmeal. Continue whisking milk and cornmeal as you slowly pour it into the boiling water. Add salt and whisk polenta until it returns to a boil and starts to thicken, about 5 minutes.

Whisk occasionally for the next 40 minutes, and a little more often during the next 10 minutes. During the final 10 minutes of cooking, stir continuously until the polenta mounds on the whisk but is still moist and pourable. Total cooking time is 60 to 65 minutes.

Meanwhile, make the stew. Blanch green beans in boiling salted water for 3 to 4 minutes, or until tender but still a little crisp. Drain and spread on tea towel.

Heat olive oil in a large sauté pan. Add green onions and sauté over low heat for a few minutes. Add bell peppers and sea salt, and sauté until tender. In the last 5 minutes of cooking, add pear or cherry tomatoes. Let cook until tomatoes start to soften a little and a few burst and exude their juices. Finally, add green beans and cook until just warmed through. Taste for salt.

Pour polenta into a mound on a large, round serving platter with a high lip. Spoon the stew and its juices around it. Evenly top polenta with ¼ cup grated cheese. Sprinkle with a generous grinding of coarse black pepper and a scattering of basil leaves torn into fragments. Place remaining cheese at the table.

tortino of parmesan and white truffles

The following recipe, translated by me, comes from Sophia Loren's cookbook *In Cucina con Amore*. It should be recited aloud in a lovely, lilting, very refined Italian accent.

If you love Parmesan cheese, and also love truffles, you'll discover that combining them creates a real explosion of flavor, and a truly extraordinary dish.

In a buttered pie dish, arrange one layer of thinly sliced white truffles; top the truffles with a layer of thinly sliced Parmesan cheese; then another layer of truffles, another layer of Parmesan. You can even do three layers, if the idea sounds appealing to you. Bathe it all in olive oil, send it into the oven, just for a few minutes, only the time it takes for the cheese to begin to soften and fuse with the truffles.

If the dish seems a little heavy, you can adjust it like this: Make some polenta and form it into a nice round, about a centimeter high, and use as the first layer; then on top of this layer of polenta, arrange the cheese and truffles. I don't know, maybe it's even better this way.

refrigerator preserves and fruit "candy"

283.

refrigerator marmalades, jams, and conserves

The following refrigerator preserves are simple concoctions, designed to be made in small batches, and "preserved" for about 1 month in the refrigerator. They require no canning in the traditional sense, or any specialized equipment—just a pot and a spoon.

Citrus fruits appear frequently in these recipes, since they are high in naturally occurring pectin, the substance that promotes jelling. Quince, sour plums, and tart apples are also high in natural pectin. Lemon juice, or other acids, helps the pectin begin the thickening process. Sugar acts as a natural preservative—no doubt the original motivation for the creation of jams and jellies.

For all recipes use heavy, nonreactive pans. Select pans that are shallower than their width so as to keep the cooking time as brief as possible and maintain the fresh taste in the fruits. The pan should be approximately double the depth of the uncooked mixture, to prevent boiling over. Stir the mixture often, since sugar tends to stick to the bottom surface and burn. And skim off foam that collects on top if you want a clearer preserve.

Since the sweetness of different fruits varies, feel free to increase or reduce the amount of sugar in the recipe according to your tastes and desires. To determine amounts, do not add sugar until halfway through the cooking. Spread a little of the cooked-down fruit on a saucer and let it cool. Taste it, keeping in mind that flavors will intensify as the jam reduces. At this point, add sugar to balance flavors. Up to $1/2$ cup sugar can be added even during the final stages of cooking.

To determine when the preserve is ready to be poured into the jars, remember that the thickening and jelling process continues as the mixture cools. The mixture should cool to a thick but loose texture. Spread a little of it on a cold saucer and pop it in the freezer for a few seconds until cold. Test the consistency by running a finger through it. If it has achieved the desired thickness, the jam is ready. Take care not to overcook the mixture; the results will be rubbery and stiff and very hard to spread.

If you are interested in learning techniques for canning and preserving foods for long periods of time, there are many wonderful books that take you through the process step by step, explain in detail the principles, and familiarize you with the equipment needed.

These preserves may be simple affairs, but they are glorious—the condensed essence of pure fruit and sugar. They glisten in their jars in the refrigerator, beckoning you with their deep, rich jewellike colors.

how to tell a jam from a jelly from a marmalade

Have you ever wondered what the difference is between a jam, a jelly, and a marmalade? What are conserves? Are they the same as preserves? *The reason for the confusion* is that many of the terms are used interchangeably. There are some defining characteristics. Following are brief descriptions of each one.

Jam: a general term for fruits, usually soft fruits, boiled with sugar until thickened

Jelly: fruit juice boiled with sugar until it becomes gelatinous and nearly transparent

Marmalade: made from boiling together the pulp, and usually the sliced rinds, of fruit with sugar until it becomes jamlike. Most often made with citrus fruits, but also with apples or quince

Preserves: a general term for any fruits or vegetables prepared for long-term storage

Fruit preserves: whole or large pieces of fruits cooked in sugar

Conserves: a type of jam made with two or more fruits, usually with nuts or raisins added.

lemon carrot marmalade

This unlikely sounding tart-sweet marmalade has me hooked. Its translucent candied fragments of lemon and carrot, sparked by ginger, will keep your taste buds begging for more. Breakfast becomes a special occasion when you bring out a jar of this glossy marmalade. Or spread it thinly on close-textured buttery bread for a lively afternoon nibble.

If possible, use Meyer lemons; they have a soft perfume and are more mellow than the more readily available variety. However, either works well.

1 pound sweet carrots

2 medium lemons, preferably organic

¾ cup sugar or to taste

2 tablespoons finely chopped candied ginger

4 cups spring water

MAKES ABOUT 2 ½ CUPS

Peel carrots and grate on large hole of a four-sided grater. Place carrots in a heavy, nonreactive saucepan large enough to contain all the ingredients comfortably.

Seed and juice lemons, and finely chop entire rind. Add to saucepan along with sugar, ginger, and water. Stir with a wooden spoon.

Cook at a simmer and stir occasionally until mixture begins to thicken. Lower heat and stir frequently until juices are thick and marmalade is glossy. Total cooking time is about 1 hour.

Transfer to jars. Let cool. Cover tightly and refrigerate. Lasts up to 1 month refrigerated.

Note: Remember, marmalade continues to thicken as it cools. About halfway through the cooking, spread a small spoonful of marmalade on a saucer and put it in the freezer for a few seconds, just until it cools, to check the consistency. Later on in the cooking, repeat. Marmalade is ready when it lightly wrinkles as you move your finger through it.

spanish tomato marmalade

Imagine a tawny, almost garnet-colored marmalade tasting of sweet, rich tomato, flecked with candied bits of lemon and perfumed with sherry.

The play of tangy lemon, aromatic wine, and cooked-down dead-ripe tomatoes is unusual but completely intriguing.

Spread this marmalade thinly on good toasted bread for a special morning or afternoon treat.

2 cups peeled, seeded, and chopped red, ripe tomatoes

1 lemon, preferably organic, seeded and juiced, entire rind chopped fine

2 cups sugar

¼ cup sweet sherry, plus 2 tablespoons

MAKES ABOUT 1 ¾ CUPS

Combine all ingredients, except 2 tablespoons sherry, in a nonreactive saucepan and let rest for 2 hours at room temperature to bring out juices and activate pectin.

Bring to a boil, then cook at a simmer, stirring occasionally. As the marmalade thickens, reduce heat and stir frequently until syrupy. Cooking time is approximately 1 hour.

Off heat, stir in remaining sherry. Pour into jars and let cool. Cover tightly and refrigerate. Lasts up to 1 month refrigerated.

fig conserve with rose water

Here, I've used dried white figs, cooked until soft and plump, to make a glossy spread dotted with a constellation of minute, crunchy fig seeds. Pine nuts and walnuts enrich the rose-water scented conserve.

Spread on thickly sliced rustic bread, it tastes like a highly evolved Fig Newton just back from a trip to the Mediterranean.

½ pound plump dried white figs, or other variety of dried fig, preferably chemical-free

Spring water

½ cup sugar

½ cup walnut halves, coarsely chopped

2 tablespoons pine nuts

1 tablespoon rose water

MAKES ABOUT 2 CUPS

Cut away the stems and finely chop figs to a paste.

Place figs in saucepan, cover with water, and simmer until very soft. Add sugar and cook about 10 minutes longer, or until mixture is thick and shiny. Stir in walnuts, pine nuts, and rose water, and cook 1 minute longer.

Spoon into jars and let cool. Cover tightly and refrigerate. Lasts for up to 1 month refrigerated.

dried apricot and almond conserve

Perfectly ripe apricots taste magical—tart yet honey-sweet, with a floral perfume. Unfortunately, the season for apricots is fleeting and the chance of getting a tree-ripened apricot in most markets (farmer's markets excluded) is very slim.

This recipe uses the next best thing: dried apricots that are picked when ripe.

Most natural food stores carry unsulphured dried apricots. In appearance, they are darker than chemically treated apricots, but their flavor and health benefits make up for any perceived cosmetic shortcomings.

1 pound pitted dried apricots, preferably unsulphured, finely chopped, about 3 cups

$1/2$ cup spring water

$3/4$ cup sugar

$1/4$ cup peeled and chopped almonds

$1/4$ teaspoon almond extract

$1/4$ teaspoon vanilla extract

MAKES ABOUT 2 CUPS

Place apricots and water in a heavy saucepan. Cook, covered, until apricots are very soft, stirring occasionally. Add sugar and stir often for about 10 minutes, or until conserve thickens. Off heat, stir in almonds and extracts.

Pour conserve into jars and let cool. Cover tightly and refrigerate. Lasts for up to 1 month refrigerated.

cotognata

Cotognata is simply quince puree cooked with sugar and lemon until it becomes a thick paste. Spread in a dish to cool, it is cut into shapes, rolled in sugar, and eaten as a sweet snack.

Cotognata is quite easy and fun to make. The sugar-sparkled, amber-colored "candies," each one wrapped in a twist of wax paper, look charming all tumbled on a pretty dish.

Look for fragrant quinces that are colored a deep yellow. Farmer's markets and specialty produce stores carry them in the fall. Remember, quince must always be cooked before eating!

$1^{1}/_{2}$ pounds quince	Almond oil or a very mild-tasting oil
$^{1}/_{2}$ lemon, sliced	
$^{2}/_{3}$–1 cup sugar, plus extra for coating	

Boil the quince and lemon in water to cover until quince is tender. Drain. Cut away core and seeds. Cut quince into chunks and put through coarse screen of food mill.

In a medium-heavy saucepan, stir together quince and $^{2}/_{3}$ cup sugar. Cook over medium heat, stirring occasionally. When mixture starts to thicken, taste for sugar and add remaining amount as needed. Stir constantly until quince pulls away from sides of pan and looks glossy and translucent.

Spread on a very lightly oiled plate to a 2-inch thickness. Let cool. Cover with cheesecloth and leave in a dry place for 2 days. Turn paste over and dry an additional day.

Cut into squares, strips, or diamonds. Dredge in sugar and shake off excess. Wrap each "candy" in a small piece of wax paper and twist ends to seal. Do not refrigerate.

a favorite bread,

a pizza,

and two quick breads

291.

yeast breads

soulful bread

Bread has many lives: freshly baked and cooled, it is eaten with dinner; the next day, slightly dried out, it is grilled for bruschetta or used as a base for country soups; completely dried, it is broken up to make bread salads, turned into bread crumbs to line baking dishes, or toasted to sprinkle on pasta.

The following breads are straightforward to make. Pizza, a type of flatbread, can be ready in about an hour. In general, flatbread dough doesn't need to rise as high as other bread doughs—the name says it all.

Semolina bread, and other breads (or desserts) containing semolina, are high in protein. Semolina bread is my all-purpose bread. I slice it for sandwiches, eat it at mealtimes, grill it for bruschetta. Its rising time comes in at about a total of 3 hours.

Quick breads are just that. Made without yeast, they rely on other ingredients to lighten the texture. They are put in the oven to bake as soon as the dough is assembled.

For those of you who do not have the time or inclination to make bread, and without access to great bread bakeries, ethnic grocery stores, such as Italian, Russian, Middle Eastern, and German markets, often feature breads made in authentic ways with pure ingredients.

If all else fails, make a special trip to the nearest good bakery that produces soulful loaves, even if it requires going out of your way. I've been told by reputable people that bread freezes well. In a pinch, this may be a practical solution, although I personally do not recommend it. Buy bread in quantity, and then freeze the amount you can't immediately use over the next several days. But do let some of it dry out—I'd be lost without dried bread in the house.

I prefer to eat bread in all its stages—from fresh to a little firmer to dry—rather than freeze it. And I can assure you, in my house not a crumb ever goes to waste.

a few simple guidelines for bread making

1.

To measure flour, stir first to aerate it, then scoop into measuring cup. Do not pack down.

2.

Do not use quick-rise yeast. It is during the long rising that bread flavor develops.

3

To determine water temperature, put your finger into a pot of gently heated water. If you can count to ten before the water becomes too hot to the touch, it is at the right temperature.

4.

Knead dough gently. Forceful kneading is not only unnecessary but harmful to the dough.

5.

The kneaded dough should be soft and supple, not dry and tight. It should move under your hands like the living thing it is.

6.

Use a spray bottle to mist the hot oven just before you put in the loaf and immediately after. Moisture helps create a good, firm crust. If you never seem to get around to buying a spray bottle (like me), just spritz water in with your fingers.

7.

To keep bread, do not put it in a plastic or paper bag, since moisture trapped inside will cause the crust to soften. Simply cover the cut side with a kitchen cloth or foil.

8.

Most important, don't worry. Just dive in and take a playful attitude. Stick to one recipe and keep trying until you understand the basic principles. Bread is made every day by people all around the world. If they can do it, so can you!

handy tools for bread making

1.

A pastry scraper is helpful, but not necessary, for handling the dough and cleaning work surfaces.

2.

A pastry brush is useful for moistening loaves, but you can also use your own slightly dampened hands.

3.

Invest in a pizza stone or unglazed quarry tiles to line the oven shelf for baking. The heated surface helps re-create the characteristics of hearth-baked bread: a firm crust, superior rise, clean-baked texture, and nonoily bread bottom.

4.

A peel, which is a large wooden paddle or spatula, is used to slide risen bread or prepared pizza directly onto the stone or tiles. A floured sheet of cardboard or a floured cookie sheet without edges will also do the trick.

important notes on ingredients

1.

Keep all flour refrigerated in airtight containers or in a cool place to preserve freshness.

2.

Look in natural food stores for organic stone-ground flours and unhulled sesame seeds for better flavor and better nutrition.

3.

Golden durum flour, ground from the endosperm of hard wheat into flour as soft as powder, is used in making bread in Puglia and Sicily. It is available through mail order from Vivande (415-346-4430). Or look for semolina (preferably organic), usually labeled as pasta flour. It will have a slightly gritty quality. To make the texture powdery, put semolina, a little at a time (about ¼ cup), into a blender along with some of the unbleached white flour called for in the recipe until it turns powdery.

4.

Buy active dry yeast and keep it cool or refrigerated. It can be purchased in bulk at natural food stores. It is also sold in small packets, each containing approximately 2½ teaspoons yeast.

5.

Malt extract, available from natural food stores, is made from fermented barley; a small amount helps activate the yeast and gives the crust a golden color. Using it is optional.

6.

Spring water is very important in bread making. Tap water, with its chemical taint, interferes with the pure flavor of home-baked bread.

thoughts before starting to bake

If this is your first bread-making experience, take some time to read over the guidelines on bread making, not once, but several times, just to absorb the essentials of the process.

True learning will come, however, when you actually start to make the bread and feel the dough under your hands. For me, the excitement begins the moment I smell the yeast and watch it become creamy and alive in warm water.

sicilian bread

Okay, I'll admit that I've been partial to Semolina bread ever since I first tasted it in the elegant Palermo home of my great-aunt Rubina.

After carefully moistening each slice with olive oil and lemon juice I gobbled it down until I couldn't eat any more—and I'm usually not given to gluttony!

I highly recommend Sicilian bread for several reasons. The combination of golden durum flour and sesame seeds creates a very high-protein bread. The flavor, which is rich and warm, makes extraordinary panini and bruschetta. It is delicious lightly toasted, with or without butter and jam, in the morning for breakfast. Unembellished, it makes a delicious and nourishing afternoon snack.

2½ teaspoons (1 package) dry yeast

1½ cups lukewarm spring water

1 tablespoon extra-virgin olive oil

2 cups finely ground golden durum flour (see page 295)

2 teaspoons fine sea salt

About 1½–2 cups unbleached white flour, preferably organic

¼ cup unhulled sesame seeds

MAKES 1 LARGE LOAF

Dissolve yeast in warm water in a large bowl. Let stand for 5 to 10 minutes until creamy. Stir in olive oil.

In a small bowl, mix together golden durum flour and salt. Stir into the yeast mixture until a batter forms. Slowly stir in ½ cup white flour. Spread 1 cup white flour on a work surface and turn the dough out onto the flour. Knead lightly until dough feels silky, about 10 minutes. Work in more flour as needed, but just a very small amount at a time. The dough should feel soft and resilient.

Form the dough into a ball. Lightly oil a large bowl. Place dough in bowl, turning to coat with oil. Place bowl in a large plastic bag and tie shut, then cover with a towel. Let rise in a warm place for about 1½ hours, or until doubled in size.

Lightly flour the work surface and lift out the dough. Moisten your hands. Without kneading or punching down, shape the dough into 1 loaf.

Heavily dust a peel or baking sheet with flour. Place the loaf on the peel and lightly brush all over with

296.

water. Sprinkle generously with sesame seeds and gently press seeds into dough. Brush again with water. Cover lightly with a towel and let rise for 40 minutes, or until nearly doubled in size. Gently reshape the dough and let rest for 10 minutes.

Meanwhile, preheat oven to 425° for 30 minutes to 1 hour, with the stone or tiles on the middle rack. Spray oven with water to create steam. Carefully slide bread onto baking stone and spray again. Bake for 10 minutes, spraying with water 1 or 2 times.

Reduce heat to 400° and bake for 40 to 50 minutes, or until the loaf is golden brown and sounds hollow when you rap the bottom with your knuckle.

Remove from oven and cool on a rack.

creations and transformations

Cooking is about creating—making yogurt from milk, bread from flour and yeast; watching the transformation of foods from liquid to solid, from inert to alive. These processes imbue cooking with a spiritual quality, especially when we stop to marvel at the wonder of it all.

pizza dough

Although it's difficult to reproduce the scorched beauty and smoldering perfume of pizza made in a wood-burning oven, an excellent pizza can be made at home. With some basic equipment, you can be sliding pizzas in and out of your oven just like a Neapolitan pro. Remember, don't overload the pizza. A very light topping is the mark of authenticity.

Without toppings, pizza dough makes a wonderful flatbread—quick, easy, and very satisfying.

1¼ teaspoons or ½ packet dry yeast

¾ cup warm spring water

¾ teaspoon fine sea salt

1½ cups unbleached white flour and ½ cup golden durum flour, stirred together, or 2 cups unbleached white flour

Extra-virgin olive oil

Semolina

SERVES 4

In a large mixing bowl, stir together yeast and warm water. Let stand for 5 minutes. With a fork, stir in salt and 1 cup of the flour. Stir in additional flour, adding it in increments, until dough begins to hold together in a ragged mass. Turn dough out onto a work surface. Gradually incorporate remaining flour as needed by flouring work surface and hands as you knead dough. Knead for about 10 minutes, or until dough is somewhat firm yet pliable. If dough becomes dry, wet hands and knead lightly, repeating until dough is supple.

Place dough in a very lightly oiled bowl. Turn it in the oil until entire surface is coated in a fine flim of oil. Place bowl in a heavy plastic bag and seal airtight. Let rise for approximately 1 to 1½ hours.

Place baking stone on bottom rack of oven. Preheat oven at 500° for 30 minutes before baking.

Generously sprinkle semolina over the entire surface of the peel.

Remove dough from bowl and pat between your palms to flatten it. Begin stretching dough, pulling outward on all sides. Let rest a little if it resists. When dough is stretched quite thin, place on the peel and continue to pat and stretch it until about 12 to 14 inches in diameter. Aim for a uniformly thin dough with a very slightly raised rim. If dough tears in spots, patch it up.

Quickly add toppings. Slide pizza onto baking stone and bake for 8 to 10 minutes, or until rim is golden. Use peel as a spatula to remove pizza from oven. Immediately cut into wedges and serve.

pizza with stracchino and arugula

The following pizza has a slightly sophisticated aura due to the presence of luscious stracchino cheese and a final showering of prosciutto and arugula.

1 recipe Pizza Dough (see page 298)

½ cup freshly made tomato sauce, put through a food mill

4 ounces fresh mozzarella, thinly sliced and drained on a tea towel folded over to cover top and bottom of cheese

3 tablespoons grated Parmesan cheese

Extra-virgin olive oil

2 ounces stracchino cheese (Brie is a fine, although not exact, substitute)

2–3 slices imported prosciutto, cut into slivers

½ cup loosely packed, coarsely chopped or torn arugula leaves

SERVES 4

Prepare dough.

Place baking stone on bottom rack of oven. Preheat oven at 500° for 30 minutes before baking.

With stretched pizza on peel, quickly spoon tomato sauce over top, stopping short of rim. Top with mozzarella slices. Sprinkle with Parmesan and lightly drizzle with olive oil. Immediately slide pizza onto baking stone in hot oven. Bake for 8 to 10 minutes, or until rim is golden. During final minutes of baking, quickly slide rack out and distribute stracchino over top of pizza. Bake for a few minutes, just until cheese melts.

Using peel as a spatula, remove pizza from oven and scatter prosciutto, then arugula, over the top.

Cut into wedges and serve immediately.

twisted cornbread

This cornbread takes a few unusual twists and turns. First, it makes a detour to Italy, where it gathers fresh basil. Traditional sugar is replaced by sweet little currants and nearly caramelized red onion. Toasted pine nuts are sprinkled throughout. But it's the buttermilk, thick, creamy, yet lean, that gives away its true identity as good old-fashioned Southern cornbread.

Cornbread is always welcome for breakfast or brunch. It makes a fitting addition to a Thanksgiving meal. Dry, it makes a great turkey stuffing. As with all cornbread, eat it as soon as it emerges from the oven—tender, a little grainy, and smelling sweetly of corn.

quick breads

$^1/_2$ small red onion, finely diced, about $^1/_2$ cup

2 teaspoons extra-virgin olive oil

1 garlic clove, peeled and finely diced

1 cup currants

$^1/_2$ cup pine nuts

1 cup stone-ground cornmeal, fine textured

$^1/_2$ cup unbleached white flour

1 tablespoon baking powder

$^1/_2$ teaspoon baking soda

$^1/_2$ teaspoon fine sea salt

$^1/_2$ cup coarsely chopped basil

1$^1/_3$ cups buttermilk

2 large eggs

3 tablespoons unsalted butter, melted

MAKES ONE 8-INCH SQUARE LOAF

Preheat oven to 450° with the rack positioned in the middle.

Cook onion in olive oil in a small sauté pan, adding garlic in the last few minutes. Onions are ready when they are golden and tender. Steam currants over boiling water for 5 minutes. Drain on a tea towel. Dry-toast pine nuts in a sauté pan until golden brown.

In a mixing bowl, stir together cornmeal, flour, baking powder, baking soda, and salt. Stir in basil and pine nuts. Beat together buttermilk, eggs, and red onion mixture.

Pour melted butter into an 8-inch square baking dish. Rotate the pan until bottom and sides are coated. A pastry brush is helpful. Pour excess butter into buttermilk mixture.

Fold liquid ingredients into dry ingredients and stir very briefly. It doesn't matter if there are lumps. Pour batter into baking dish and sprinkle currants over top. Bake for 30 to 35 minutes, or until top is golden brown and a thin skewer inserted into the bread comes out clean.

Serve immediately.

wild black walnut bread

Black walnuts, native to America, were once a part of our food landscape, used in breads and ice cream, and in other dishes calling for walnuts. Like truffles, black walnuts have a strong, deep, and haunting flavor. They make English walnuts, the kind most common today, seem a bit dull.

In the following recipe, black walnuts and unrefined brown sugar make for a unique walnut bread. Wonderful in the morning with coffee or caffè latte, or eat it as an afternoon snack along with a square of black bittersweet chocolate to nibble on. Make small black walnut bread tea sandwiches by spreading thin slices with lightly sugared mascarpone. The bread also makes a delicious and appropriate addition to cool-weather holiday meals.

$2\frac{1}{2}$ cups unbleached white flour

3 teaspoons baking powder

$\frac{1}{2}$ teaspoon salt

$\frac{1}{3}$–$\frac{1}{2}$ cup unrefined brown sugar

2 large eggs, beaten

1 cup milk

1 cup chopped black walnuts (see Note)

MAKES 1 LOAF

continued

301-

Preheat oven to 300°. Butter a standard loaf pan.

In a mixing bowl, combine flour, baking powder, salt, and sugar. Use a fork to stir ingredients together. Combine beaten eggs and milk, and stir. Add all at once to dry ingredients, stirring quickly until flour is all moistened. Don't worry if lumps remain. Quickly fold in nuts, just enough to distribute them, and transfer to the loaf pan, pushing the batter into the corners.

Bake for 20 minutes. Increase heat to 375° and bake 25 to 30 minutes longer, or until the crust is golden brown and a thin skewer inserted into loaf comes out clean. Let cool for a few minutes in loaf pan, then remove from pan and cool on a rack.

Note: If black walnuts are not available in your area, they can be purchased by mail order from American Spoon Foods (800-647-2512). Of course, this bread can also be made using English walnuts, but toast them first to intensify their flavor.

Fresh desserts

303.

on ending a meal

As much as we love desserts, overly rich and complicated pastries, creams, and cakes have no place at the end of a meal. They are more suited to fancy parties, special celebrations, or enjoyed in the afternoon at a café with an espresso.

It has been said many times: Fruit is the best way to end a meal. A single type of fruit—served whole, the way nature created it—tree-ripened, with a full bouquet and luscious flesh, brings any meal to a spectacular finish. Don't underestimate the seductive power of a bowl of gorgeous blushing peaches, a dish of cold, soft persimmons, or heady strawberries deep scarlet through and through.

Many of the recipes offered here consist of fruit, either a single one or an assemblage; fruits and nuts; or fruits and fresh, lean ricotta. For the most part, no cooking is involved; the only "work" is in selecting ripe, fragrant fruit, fresh nutmeats, and finely crafted ricotta and confections. And that is a pleasure.

You'll notice that I've devoted several pages to the making of fruit "salads." The word *salad* in regard to fruits bothers me, since it conjures up images of some rather sorry fruit salads that usually make the rounds. However, the mingled flavors and scents of a carefully made fruit salad add up to something of a miracle; the combined juices taste like nectar reserved for the deities. I prefer the word "macedonia" to describe a salad of mixed fruits. The word, with its bit of mystery, is more evocative of the delight that awaits us.

Think of the following desserts as extensions of the meal. They play an important role in providing us with the *full* range of foods we all want to be eating—and fruit figures prominently on that list.

These sweet endings can also serve as integral components of the meal itself. For example, top off a simple supper of leafy green salad and rough country bread with a piece of fresh fruit and a little dish of cool, nutritious rum-flavored ricotta. In winter, roasted walnuts, hot from the oven, can end a meal of vegetable soup on a deeply flavorful note of sustenance.

peaches in asti spumante

Serving peaches in wine, most often red wine, is a long-standing custom in the Mediterranean.

But pour chilled Asti Spumante over peaches and it becomes a special-occasion dessert. Asti Spumante, an Italian sparkling wine made from muscat grapes, has a floral fragrance and honeyed flavor that amplify the peach essence.

The lush orange flesh of peach slices looks absolutely gorgeous immersed in the pale gold fizzy wine. Or use sugary, white-fleshed Babcock or Indian Red peaches for a delicate pastel dessert. Be forewarned that Babcock peaches bruise very easily, so handle them with utmost care.

| Ripe peaches, any variety | Chilled best-quality Asti Spumante |
| Sugar to taste | |

If the peaches are dead ripe, you can often strip the skin off with a knife. Or dip the peaches for a few seconds in boiling water. Peel the fruit and slice directly into wide-mouthed goblets or dessert dishes. Sprinkle with a little sugar and let rest a few minutes. Pour enough cold Asti Spumante over peaches to cover. Serve immediately.

cherries and almonds

Cherries and almonds are one of the great fruit and nut pairings, each enhancing the other in a very special way.

Almonds are at the "green" stage in June—when the hull is tender and light green, and the nut is white and moist—before the shell hardens and the nut dries out. And June is when cherries flood the markets. So they are naturally friendly companions.

When green almonds aren't available, offer raw, unpeeled almonds.

Look for plump, deeply colored Bing and Royal Ann cherries and select each cherry individually.

Cherries and almonds look lovely served in old-fashioned bowls or straw baskets lined with green leaves.

Ripe Bing or Royal Ann cherries	Green almonds or raw, unpeeled almonds, preferably Mission variety

Arrange cherries and almonds in separate bowls or baskets.

If serving green almonds, offer small knives to cut through the soft shell. Each almond is then easily peeled. Unpeeled dry almonds need only be popped into one's mouth.

frutta e verdura

The final recipe in my book *Verdura* is for an Italian offering called *sopratavola*, a selection of raw fruits and vegetables known specifically to cool and refresh the body, lightly sweeten the mouth, and aid digestion.

The combination of fruits and vegetables is to my mind one of the finest ways to end any meal. The fresh, sweet juices, mineral essences, mingled soft earthy scents, and absence of pretense are at the very heart of what eating well is all about.

Select from the following and use only what is in season.

Small, flawless fennel bulbs with feathery tops	Grape clusters (grapes with seeds have greater flavor and deeper perfumes)
Very fresh celery hearts topped with leaves	Melon
Small crisp radishes with fresh green leaves	Cucumbers, small Armenian or English, peeled and cut into thick strips

Trim away some of the fennel tops and pare away any surface blemishes on base of stalks. Trim base of celery in the same way. Cut fennel and celery lengthwise into quarters or eighths.

Remove all but one or two leaves on the top of each radish or if the leaves are not perfect, trim them all off. Wash radishes very thoroughly.

With scissors, cut grapes into good-sized clusters.

Peel and seed melon, and cut into wedges.

Wrap cucumber strips, fennel, celery, and radishes in damp tea towels. Place grape clusters and melon wedges in a bowl. Keep fruits and vegetables in a cool place or refrigerate until needed.

To serve, arrange fruits and vegetables in a shallow bowl. Serve slightly cool.

enchanting apricots

They do seem to cast a spell. Fully tree-ripened apricots are almost too good to be true. Bad apricots are those picked before they are ripe and doomed never to develop their magical flavor and richly sweet juices.

For years I searched and searched in vain for good apricots. In fact, the apricots that are widely available commercially made me feel so angry at being cheated by those meddling with nature that I stopped buying them altogether.

I lived in fear that I would lose the precious memory of the true apricot flavor until a few years ago, when I lived in the country and once again was able to pick ripe apricots off a tree.

These days, farmer's markets offer truly ripe apricots. But the season is fleeting—mid to late June for the old-fashioned heirloom varieties such as Royal Blenheim, Moorpark, and Derby Royal. These are the apricots I remember from my childhood, full of flavor and scent, that grow in the side yards of old houses. The newer varieties are larger, harder, and more acidic—they will disappoint you every time.

Most apricots need to ripen until the flesh is quite soft but still intact—just at the point before they turn liquid. Moorpark apricots are richly flavored and meaty, even when the apricots appear slightly underripe.

apricot sauce

Tree-ripened apricots have a brilliant orange color and a honey-sweet taste that has just a hint of lemon. If you have searched hard to find apricots that recall those of childhood—and are as enraptured by the flavor as I am—you will probably want to eat them immediately, just as they are. However, if you are blessed with an abundant source of ripe apricots, you can make this luscious sauce to serve with Dessert Rice Cake (see page 322), which serves as a creamy backdrop to the apricot flavor.

¾ pound fresh ripe apricots, pitted and coarsely cut into pieces	Spring water
	2 tablespoons sugar (see Note)
½ vanilla bean	**MAKES ABOUT 1 CUP**

Place apricots and vanilla bean in a saucepan. Add enough water to come a little less than halfway up the apricots. Gently simmer for 20 minutes, or until the juices thicken and a chunky sauce forms. A few minutes before sauce is ready, sprinkle with sugar and stir.

Note: Apricot skins toughen when cooked with sugar, therefore add sugar toward end of cooking.

artificial extracts

Imitation vanilla extract, like all imitation flavors, is composed of chemical compounds that attempt to reproduce an essence. In fact, they fail entirely to do so.

This fraudulent product has none of the mystery of true vanilla beans. It is strident and banal at the same time, with a one-dimensional flavor.

Chemical flavorings added to foods create a distorted, sickly impression of the taste—rather than a deep, clearly delineated yet softly seductive flavor. And needless to say, the harmful ingredients they contain should be avoided.

marinated fresh figs

Figs that have basked in the sun until they start to split from the fullness of their honeyed juices are the ones to use here.

I can't think of a more refreshing way to enjoy them than briefly macerated in sweetened orange juice and crushed mint leaves, and served very cold. The purple-black peel of Mission figs tints the juices blush-pink.

Use any variety of fresh tree-ripened fig—Brown Turkey with red flesh, violet-fleshed Kadota, and others. What is crucial is that the figs be plump and juicy. Avoid dried or withered-looking figs, or those that feel hard to the touch.

12 ripe figs	Sugar to taste
Juice of 2 large, juicy oranges	12 mint leaves
Juice of 1 lemon	**SERVES 3 TO 4**

Trim stems from figs. On stem end, make 2 incisions to form a cross going one third of the way down the fig. Place figs upside down in a shallow white bowl large enough to contain them in 1 layer. Press each fig down lightly to anchor it.

In a small bowl, combine citrus juices. Add sugar and stir until sugar dissolves. Pour juices over figs. Lightly bruise 6 mint leaves between your fingers and plunge them into the juices.

Refrigerate until well chilled. Bring bowl to table. To serve, place 3 to 4 figs, cut side up, on serving dishes. Spoon juices over the top. Sprinkle with remaining mint leaves torn into large fragments.

fresh figs with almond and chocolate stuffing

When embellishing a ripe fig one must take care not to intrude upon its sublime flavor and texture. Here, I've assembled a highly complementary trio of flavors—chocolate, almonds, and rum—and used them in a filling for fresh figs. Think of this as a cross between fresh fruit and fine chocolates.

The flavor of these figs stayed in my mind for days—like the memory of a happy dream.

¾ cup finely chopped raw, unpeeled almonds	12 ripe, juicy figs
2 tablespoons finely chopped bittersweet chocolate	
1 tablespoon dark rum, or enough to lightly bind almonds and chocolate into a paste	**SERVES 4**

Place almonds and chocolate in a bowl and stir together. Pour in rum and stir until mixture just holds together. Add a few more drops of rum if necessary.

Trim stems from figs. Starting at stem end, cut figs ¾ of the way down, making 2 incisions in the form of a cross. Carefully pinch bottoms of figs, which will cause tops to open like a flower.

Gently mound almond mixture into the center of each fig. Press fig together to reshape. Arrange on a platter and serve.

frutta e ricotta alla romana

At the end of a meal, offer fruit and ricotta as the Romans do. Arrange the fruits in a basket, and serve the ricotta accompanied by little dishes of cocoa, sugar, cinnamon, and ground espresso so that each person can mix in whatever they desire.

Served al fresco on a balmy summer evening, this dessert creates a dreamy *la dolce vita* feeling.

Creamy ricotta, preferably from an artisanal producer	Dutch-process cocoa, finely ground espresso, ground cinnamon, and sugar
Ripe summer fruits, such as peaches, figs, plums, and apricots	

Wrap ricotta in several layers of cheesecloth and place in a colander to drain off excess moisture. Refrigerate until needed.

To serve, mound ricotta on a platter and place on the table. Spoon cocoa, espresso, cinnamon, and sugar in little piles around the ricotta, or offer in small dishes. Accompany with washed fruits arranged in a basket.

Provide plates, knives, and forks. Each person selects a fruit and slices it, then takes a big spoonful of ricotta and flavors it to taste. The ricotta can either be spread on the sliced fruit or the fruit dipped into the ricotta.

eating persimmons.

For the first four years of my life, my family
lived in a semirural town in presuburban southern California.
Our garden was a wild green place all tangled up with morning
glories and bordered by an old-fashioned wire fence that lent
itself to neighborly conversations. The trees in the backyard
bore so much fruit that the ground would become sticky with
rotting fruit, the air almost sickly sweet.

In the fall hundreds of heart-shaped, burnt-orange fruits
dangled from the branches of the persimmon tree, the biggest
tree in the yard. We would eat the persimmons when they were
dead ripe. The sweet jellylike flesh would slip down my throat
and sometimes leave a strange "furry" feeling in my mouth
when I ate the flesh right next to the skin.

A persimmon tree in autumn is a sight to behold—the
scaly white-gray bark; the large, dusty-green leaves blushed
with rose; then later a stunning absence of leaves; and large
jewellike fruits against a brilliant blue or gray and brooding sky.

To fully enjoy a persimmon, ripen it at room temperature
until quite soft, then refrigerate. When it is nice and cold, pop
out the stem end, cut the fruit in half, and eat it out of hand,
taking care to avoid the "furry" sensation!

fresh persimmon sauce

Ripe persimmons, with their sweet, glistening flesh and brilliant orange color are unique.

Use this simple, uncooked, lemon-accented persimmon sauce to top vanilla ice cream; my preference is for a little ice cream and a lot of persimmon sauce.

Thanks to Myrna Canbianica, my friend in beautiful Ojai, for sharing this recipe with me. She makes the sauce with persimmons and lemons from her garden.

2 Hachiya persimmons, ripened until very soft	1 teaspoon lemon juice
Zest of ½ small lemon, preferably organic	

Peel persimmons. Mash flesh to a chunky puree. Stir in lemon zest and juice. Cover and chill. Serve over ice cream.

sweet rum ricotta

A simple dessert to assemble, but the ricotta and rum reward you with great flavor and a wonderful creamy texture.

Serve in little goblets for dessert. It also makes a very nutritious and discreetly indulgent afternoon snack.

8 ounces whole milk ricotta	3 tablespoons sugar
3 tablespoons rum	**SERVES 2**

For a smooth texture, push ricotta through the fine screen of a food mill. For a more rustic texture, simply stir with a flat wooden spoon or fork.

Combine rum and sugar in a small bowl. Stir until sugar melts, a matter of a few minutes. Stir sweetened rum into ricotta until all liquid is absorbed.

Cover and refrigerate for several hours or overnight to let the ricotta flavors "ripen."

tangerines and espresso

Is it possible to pass on a sensory memory? Mine is only the memory of a memory and can never compare to the sharpness with which my mother experiences it. But I, too, have a picture in my mind of my great-grandmother sitting at the table in her elegant dining room, sipping dark espresso from a tiny cup and peeling a brilliant tangerine, to end the meal during cold Palermo winters— even though she died before I was born.

For my mother, the scent of tangerines instantly and always brings to mind this image.

| Finely ground espresso beans | Tangerines, very sweet and juicy, |
| Spring water | preferably organic |

Prepare the coffee with espresso beans and spring water. Use a stovetop Moka espresso maker or an espresso machine, if you have one.

Place tangerines on a small plate. Pour freshly brewed espresso into a demitasse cup. Peel tangerines and eat tangerine segments between sips of espresso.

the fate of apples

Apples held in cold storage suffer terribly, and many of those in supermarkets are the victims of just such a fate. The ability of an apple to be held in cold storage and shipped often determines which varieties are produced.

Apples produced on a large scale are bred to be fairly bland in order to appeal to the largest number of people. As a result spicy-sweet flavor, deep perfume, crisp flesh are sacrificed. Supermarket apples are large and perfect and shiny, but utterly disappointing, with mealy flesh and weak flavor.

Freshly picked apples from small farms bear very little resemblance to the uniform super-market monsters. Instead, each apple has subtle variations in shape; the skins are matte and may be speckled or streaked, tender or rough, and are rust-colored, pale ocher, or green; the flesh may be colored ivory, pale gold, or light pink. When you bite into them, they crackle and burst with juice.

These apples, many of which I never knew existed, have awakened in me a love of the fruit. If your interest in apples has waned, I urge you to seek out unusual, heirloom specimens. Historically, there have been over seven thousand varieties of apples recorded in the United States alone. Why should we limit ourselves to only four or five uninspired ones and forsake the rest?

apples and roasted walnuts

Cool, crisp apples and warm roasted walnuts make me think of autumn leaves and woodsmoke, and for good reason. Walnuts are freshly harvested in the fall, a time when many apples are at their peak.

Offer apples and walnuts at the end of a country-style meal or as an afternoon snack. Shelling nuts and eating apples is a very calming activity.

Do not refrigerate apples; simply keep them in a cool place.

New-crop walnuts in the shell | Crisp seasonal apples

Place unshelled walnuts on a cookie sheet and roast in a 400° oven for 12 to 15 minutes.

Serve hot walnuts and cool apples in separate bowls or baskets. If serving at the end of a meal, provide plates, knives, and nutcrackers. For a snack, just a nutcracker and a napkin will do.

ice cream with orange sauce

Remember the orange and vanilla ice cream bars on a stick, sold from musical trucks that roamed our suburban streets in summertime? I always loved the contrast of creamy vanilla and tart-sweet orange.

Here, freshly squeezed orange juice and a big spoonful of vanilla ice cream are stirred together into a sauce for a little dish of vanilla ice cream to be eaten on a hot and lazy afternoon.

Warning: You may become seized with the desire to go running wildly through the backyard sprinklers. That's how I spent many a blissful summer day when I was a child.

Oranges | Best-quality vanilla ice cream

Juice 1 orange for every serving of ice cream. With a fork, blend the orange juice with enough ice cream to form a creamy sauce.

Scoop the ice cream into a well-chilled ice cream dish or small goblet. Spoon the sauce over the top and eat immediately.

frutta, noci, e confettura

For a lovely ending to a fall or winter meal, just assemble some wonderful seasonal foods: fruits, nuts, and sweet confections.

The communal aspects of this offering are especially important. Everyone serves themselves from a large wicker tray. This encourages relaxation and spending time at the table in leisurely conversation.

Crack the nuts and pick out the meats, slowly savor pieces of juicy pear, peel a perfumed tangerine. These are all meditative acts that help us to slow down the mad pace of life.

Seek out torrone and panforte in Italian markets. In season, you can make the cotognata (quince paste) yourself or purchase it ready-made at Italian, Latino, or Middle Eastern markets.

Choose from the following; or offer them all, for a very special, lavish, and beautiful display.

Small pears, tangerines, and other seasonal fruits

Moist dates, dried apricots, and other high-quality dried fruits without preservatives

New-crop walnuts in the shell

Cotognata (see page 290)

Torrone (almond nougat)

Panforte (a flattened, spiced confection of nuts and candied citrus rind)

Arrange ingredients on a wicker tray or trays. Provide individual dessert plates, knives, and forks.

Dessert Rice Cake

Sweet and creamy, with the chewiness of Arborio rice, this dandy little cake is great with caffè latte in the morning, for an afternoon nibble and of course, for dessert.

Use that dried bread you've been saving and make bread crumbs to line the pan.

2¹/₂ cups lean milk	4 eggs, separated
³/₄ cup Arborio rice	6 tablespoons sugar
Fine sea salt	Unsalted butter and fine bread crumbs, unseasoned
6 tablespoons finely ground almonds (use a hand-cranked cheese grater)	
Zest of 1 lemon, preferably organic	**SERVES 6**

Bring milk to a boil in a heavy saucepan. Add rice and a small pinch of salt, and stir for a few minutes. Simmer for about 10 minutes. Then stir regularly until the milk is almost all absorbed into the rice.

Let cool, then stir in almonds and lemon zest. Slowly incorporate beaten egg yolks, then stir in sugar.

Butter an 8¹/₂-inch cake pan and line with bread crumbs. Shake out excess.

Beat egg whites until they form stiff peaks and gently fold into rice mixture. Quickly pour into prepared cake pan. Bake at 400° for 30 minutes, or until a thin wooden skewer inserted into cake comes out clean. Let rest a few minutes and then unmold.

poor little kiwi

What did the innocent little kiwi do to end up being so publicly humiliated, mocked, and scorned, the laughingstock of the food world?

This hairy little green-fleshed fruit traveled to our country from New Zealand, suitcase in hand, hoping for a little acceptance. It's not the fault of the kiwi that chefs went a little mad.

That sparkling green flesh was its undoing. And its supremely refreshing balance of sweet and tart; its ring-shaped constellation of tiny, crunchy black seeds; the paper-thin skin, so easily peeled.

Let's welcome it anew, since kiwis are too good to discard on the slag heap of life. Let's allow its dull brown skin to fool us again, let's be surprised once more at its glistening green flesh. When we taste it, let it be like the first time.

A kiwi must be allowed to ripen properly. It should be as soft as a ripe peach, to develop its sugar and cause the juices to form. Peel it. Eat it, and enjoy it forever.

If fruit salad seems boring, I urge you to read on.

True, salads made with insipid, unripe fruits *aren't* very exciting. Perhaps some of you associate fruit salad with the canned kind, small, pale cubes of indistinguishable fruits immersed in a sickly sweet liquid, all with the same insipid texture and faint flavor except for those indestructible maraschino cherries.

Now, forget those canned fruit salads, deli fruit salads in styrofoam bowls wrapped in plastic, salad-bar fruit salads, and any that are prepared without care and attention.

As a first step to creating a truly great salad, you must learn to recognize and select good fruit in the market. Is the fruit aromatic? Is it gently yielding? Is it a good variety? And, most important, is it in season?

Once you've gathered together good fruit, most of the work is done. Here are a few tips for preparing individual fruits.

peaches, nectarines, apricots, plums: Cut along the natural division of soft summer fruit and make slices along the pit. Peaches usually require peeling; very ripe ones can be stripped of their skin with a paring knife. Otherwise, simply dip peaches in boiling water for a few seconds, then strip off the skin. Nectarines, apricots, and plums have soft, thin skins and do not require peeling. Slice fruit or cut them into dice.

cherries: Buy an inexpensive cherry pitter (about $2). With this little tool, you can pit cherries easily. They will spurt a little juice, so wear an old apron or old clothes. Keep in mind that juices from cut cherries will tint the salad pink.

figs: Ripe figs are very soft and must be treated with great care. Trim stem ends. Slice lengthwise into quarters and add to fruit salad just before serving.

apples: Peel and core apples. Dice into salad and quickly mix with macerating juices to prevent discoloring, or toss diced apples in a little lemon juice first to preserve color.

pears: Use firm, ripe pears. Peel and core. Dice into macerating juices or toss in a little lemon juice to prevent discoloration.

mangoes: Wonderfully perfumed fruit with dense, velvety flesh. Peel thickly with a vegetable peeler and cut flesh in bite-size pieces, working your way toward the pit.

papayas: Peel thickly, cut in half, and scoop out black seeds. Dice flesh. Look for huge red-fleshed papayas in Latino markets.

melons: Cantaloupe, honeydew, Persian, Sharlyn, and other small melons with soft skins. Peel melons with a knife, cut in half, and scoop out the seeds. Dice.

watermelon: Cut away thick rind and whitish flesh near rind. Dice flesh and pick out seeds. Add to rest of fruit salad mix just before serving to preserve its crisp texture.

berries: Blackberries and raspberries: Discard any berries that are starting to deteriorate. Wash gently by dipping into a bowl of cool water, then drain well on clean old tea towels. Excess water on berries will dilute salad juices. Add whole berries to mix. Strawberries: Wash berries gently before hulling. Drain, then insert a paring knife into the hull and cut away the entire cone-shaped section. Cut small strawberries in half lengthwise, larger ones in quarters.

oranges: If you've despaired of trying to make perfect orange segments, here's an easy and efficient way to do it, culled from Elizabeth David's cookbooks.

First, slice the unpeeled orange into eighths lengthwise. Then, working over a dish, cut away the thick peel and let the sections fall into the bowl. Reserve the peels. Squeeze any juice out of the peels into the bowl with the orange segments. Blood oranges add a special touch to a fruit salad.

bananas: This fruit has become as familiar as peanut butter and jelly. But, a banana is an amazing fruit—tropical, creamy, and softly perfumed. On the Pacific coast below Santa Barbara, there is an organic banana farm that grows banana varieties with extraordinary nuances of flavor, such as pineapple or custard. For fruit mixes I especially recommend small red bananas—firm, lush, with perfumed pink flesh. Regular yellow bananas are delicious, too. Simply peel fruit and cut into small chunks.

grapes: Grapes contribute little bursts of liquid sweetness. It is tempting to add seedless grapes to a mix, but they are less flavorful and less perfumed than seeded varieties. It's worth the extra time to cut grapes in half and seed them. I recommend muscat grapes, sometimes called Italia or Italian grapes, for their sweet, flowery taste. Intensely spicy-sweet Concord grapes, called slipskins since the skin slips right off when squeezed, are delicious but it is difficult to pick out the seeds. Better eaten out of hand, since the seeds are much more easily spit out!

lemons and limes: Lemon and lime juice is added to macedonias to point up the sweetness of the fruits and give them sparkle.

other fruits: Other fruits that can be added to macedonia include pineapple; kiwis; crisp, sweet Fuyu persimmons; fresh dates; and prickly pears.

fruits in kirschwasser

As you add each layer of fruit to the serving bowl, sprinkle it with sugar and moisten with kirschwasser, a strong, clear cherry brandy. The lightly syrupy juice that forms in the bowl tastes like the distilled essence of summer. Maraschino liqueur or a dessert wine of high quality, such as Essencia or Moscato d'Asti, would also be lovely.

As you sugar each layer, keep in mind the degree of sweetness of the wine or spirit you select as well as the natural sugar content of the fruits.

See pages 323–326 for guidance in selecting and preparing fruits.

2 peaches, preferably white	Handful raspberries
Sugar	A few freshly peeled green almonds, split along the natural division, about 1/4 cup
Kirschwasser	
4 apricots	
2 plums, preferably with red flesh	
2 small red bananas with pink flesh, if available, or 1 yellow banana	**SERVES 4 TO 6**

Peel peaches. Slice peaches along the natural division, working your way around the pit. Cut slices into bite-size pieces. Add peaches to serving bowl. Sprinkle with sugar and drizzle with kirschwasser. Slice unpeeled apricots and plums in the same way, sugaring and moistening each layer as you add it to the bowl. Chill for about 30 minutes.

Gently stir in bananas. Sprinkle with raspberries and almonds.

berries—how to store and clean

Freshly picked ripe berries are extremely fragile and short-lived. If possible, use the berries within a day or two of gathering or purchase.

Spread berries out in a single layer on a large plate or on sheets of wax paper; piled on top of each other (the way they are in plastic market "baskets") they become moldy extremely quickly. Don't refrigerate them unless you want to extend their life beyond a couple of days—cold temperatures dull the flavors.

Washing berries is a delicate job. A strong jet of water, or too much exposure to water, can destroy their integrity. If you know the origin of the berries and are sure they are completely organic, it is preferable not to wash them, since water can dilute the flavor and impair the texture a bit.

In most other cases, play it safe and give the berries just a brief cleansing. Drop a few into a bowl of cool water and gently swish them around. Lift out each berry, letting excess water drain back into bowl. Place in one layer on clean old tea towels to absorb excess water.

a few special drinks
and a healing tea

329.

donna santa's concord grape juice

This recipe comes from Donna Santa, a friend of the family, who maintained a beautiful Italian garden at her home in southern California. She served her homemade Concord grape juice in tall glasses filled with ice, and offered her own crunchy, lightly sweet, anise biscotti.

We drank the fragrant, dark purple juice and crunched on the licorice-scented cookies in the shade of her *pergolata*, a grape arbor of dappled green light. Before leaving, she used to pick for us lavish bouquets of fragrant pink and red roses and glorious red amaryllis.

Concord grapes can be purchased at farmer's markets and specialty produce markets from late summer through early October.

Concord grapes	
Colander	
Cheesecloth	**1 QUART GRAPES YIELDS 2 CUPS JUICE**

Wash grapes well and remove stems. Place grapes in a saucepan and crush with a wooden spoon. Bring juices to a boil, stirring occasionally. Be careful not to let grapes or juices burn.

Line a colander with 2 layers of dampened cheesecloth. Strain grapes through cheesecloth. Form cheesecloth into a ball and, wearing rubber gloves to prevent staining your hands, squeeze cheesecloth to extract all the juice.

Transfer grape juice to a clean saucepan and bring to a boil. Pour into sterilized glass jars and seal. If you plan to drink the grape juice during the next few days, simply let the grape juice come to room temperature and refrigerate. If desired, accompany with homemade or store-bought anise biscotti.

fresh watermelon juice

There are many foods I associate with my father—but the one that is closest to my heart is watermelon. He loved watermelon since the days of his Italian boyhood.

I, too, have a passionate love of watermelon. To me, other melons seem cloying and heavy compared with watermelon's thirst-quenching light and sugary juices and crisp red flesh.

My father would always select and ready the watermelon for the family, carefully cutting it into bite-size dice and meticulously removing every seed. He was a master judge of watermelons. I can still see the sparkle in his eyes and the look of pure, childlike happiness that came over his face when he cut into a crisp, juicy melon with sweet red flesh. A mealy, pale-fleshed, or less-than-sweet melon would cause genuine disappointment.

Sometimes, despite your best efforts, the watermelon turns out to be soft and mealy. If the flesh is sweet, I simply turn it into juice to make a refreshing, and deep pink drink. I know my father would approve.

3½ pounds watermelon
Sugar, only if needed | **MAKES 1 QUART**

Cut watermelon rind away from flesh, making sure to remove all the pale flesh close to the rind and reserve only the red portions. Cut watermelon into chunks. Remove any clusters of seeds you see, but don't worry about any that may remain.

Put chunks, in 3 batches, through the finest screen of a food mill. Make sure to rotate the handle both clockwise and counterclockwise. Strain through several layers of dampened cheesecloth. Taste and, if not pleasingly sweet, stir in a touch of sugar. Chill until very cold. Do not use ice cubes, since they weaken the strength of the delicate juice as they melt.

red wine punch king louis XIV

This is a rich red wine infused with crushed almonds, paper-thin apple slices, hot red pepper, and exotic spices.

I've adapted this wonderful recipe from Maurice Mességué's *C'est la Nature Qui a Raison*. Published in 1972, it is an impassioned and lyrical treatise on the importance of reconnecting with nature and rediscovering its healing powers, as well as a cautionary tale about the dangers of pollutants in modern life.

This punch has a magical aura about it. A warning (or a promise): It is highly potent. Serve in small cupfuls.

1 quart full-bodied red wine

1¼ cups sugar

2 thin slices fresh hot red pepper or ⅛ teaspoon hot red pepper flakes

1 apple, peeled, cored, and sliced paper-thin

12 coarsely crushed raw almonds (crushing releases sweet oils)

3 slices fresh or dried ginger

12 cloves

One 2-inch stick cinnamon

SERVES 8

Pour red wine into a deep bowl. Add sugar and stir with a wooden spoon. Add remaining ingredients and stir well. Cover tightly and let steep for at least 24 hours or for several days, in or out of the refrigerator (the sugar acts as a preservative). Strain through several layers of dampened cheesecloth. Ladle into punch cups or small glasses.

nectar

This honey and brandy drink will make you feel you've traveled back to antiquity, especially if you prepare it in an earthenware jar.

According to the rules of the Greek gods, this concoction must mellow for 10 years before drinking. But I consider it to be ambrosial after a mere 24 hours.

1 quart spring water	½–1 cup brandy
12 ounces organic honey	**MAKES 6 SMALL SERVINGS**

Boil together the water and honey for about 25 minutes, or until reduced by half. Pour into an earthenware jar or pitcher and let cool. Add brandy, varying amount depending on desired strength. Stir with a wooden spoon. Cover with a cloth. Let rest for at least 24 hours. Stir before serving.

stina's healing tea

"Sans herbs, Stina insisted she could neither cook nor even live, and there was scarcely a night in the year that she did not brew herself a tisane of chamomile. Let one of us but sneeze, and there was set before us a steaming infusion of mint, sweet marjoram, sweet basil, and sage, steeped with honey and slices of lemon, and spiked with brandy—Stina's unfailing preventative and cure for colds." (From *Stina,* by Herman Smith, 1942, in the chapter titled "The First Violets.")

Here is my recipe for this delicious tea. I've made it many times and it has saved me from getting a cold—its fragrance and flavor immediately lift my spirits. The herbs have many beneficial properties, such as the natural antibiotic in sage.

1 sprig each sage, basil, marjoram, and spearmint

1 thin slice lemon, preferably organic

1 cup spring water

$^1/_2$ teaspoon honey

2 teaspoons brandy

SERVES 1

Simmer together herbs, lemon, and water for 10 to 15 minutes. Stir in honey, cover, and let steep for 5 minutes. Stir in brandy and drink.

Essential pantry.

335.

If you strip my pantry down to the items that are absolutely essential to cooking, this is what you will find:

Bottled spring water

Fine and coarse sea salt from the Mediterranean

Black peppercorns

Dried small hot red peppers and hot red pepper flakes

Ground espresso

Extra-virgin olive oil from Mediterranean countries, including the extraordinary olive oil from Puglia and a buttery-tasting one from Lebanon

Boxes of imported Italian dried pasta

Rice—Arborio and basmati

A variety of dried beans—from the recent harvest

Organic canned beans, especially chick peas (they hold up better than other types)

Organic canned tomatoes or imported canned San Marzano tomatoes

Dried bread (made without oils or butter, bread dries without becoming moldy or rancid)

Lemons

Garlic and onions

demystifying extra-virgin olive oil

Despite the fact that it sounds somewhat intimidating, extra-virgin olive oil is a basic and simple product, as natural as sea salt, as pure as sweet water—and as old as time.

To make it, olives are gathered at a certain specific point in their maturity. First they are crushed into a paste. Then the paste is placed under weights to force out the oil. No damaging heat is used to encourage the olives to release their oil and no chemicals are involved. The process is not mysterious, nor is it very complicated. What is essential is the quality of the olives and the integrity of the producer.

Good extra-virgin olive oil has an "alive" quality to its flavor. The flavor expands in your mouth in the way that wine does; bring your nose close and the scent reveals itself like a perfumed flower in bloom on a hot day. Not heavy or viscous, it is miraculously light on your tongue, never leaving an oily residue—the mark of bad oil.

What is labeled simply as "olive oil" is not a pure and natural product. It doesn't belong in a kitchen where careful, healthy cooking is taking place.

Yes, extra-virgin olive oil costs more than industrially produced vegetable oils. But it is so much more than just a cooking medium. It brings depth of flavor to foods; it elevates humble ingredients. Like magic, a thin trickle of glinting golden olive oil in food has transformational powers. And it has health-giving properties. It is the very soul of many of the recipes in this book.

I wish I could say all extra-virgin olive oils are equally good. But, like wine, quality varies. Keep tasting oils until you have a basic understanding of the range of flavors—buttery, tasting of artichokes, warm and nutty, tasting green and grassy, sharp and peppery, ripe and fruity, and so forth—and degrees of "weight," until you fall in love with an olive oil's particular and unique personality.

Each time you taste truly fine olive oil, it fills your senses. So drizzle a little on a crust of bread, close your eyes, and let the seduction begin.

sea salt, coarse and fine

Salt is the only mineral used in cooking. Without it we could not survive; hence the importance placed on it as a commodity in many countries around the world.

For a vibrant taste and pure, fresh scent use sea salt. Sea salt has no additives. In cooking, I use various kinds from Greece, Sicily, France, Lebanon, and other countries.

Fine sea salt is all-purpose, but is especially good on salads and other uncooked dishes that are served right away, since coarse salt crystals would not melt immediately. The coarse crystals also cause tender leaves to wilt and blacken.

Coarse salt is best used for drawing the moisture and bitter juices out of raw eggplant; when a dish is cooked slowly, which melts the salt; or for sprinkling over focaccia before baking. Coarse salt can be ground in a mortar for a finer texture.

Remember, since sea salt is pure, it is potent, so you need to use less than you would of so-called table or pouring salt.

black peppercorns, heat and scent

Always buy whole black peppercorns. Grind them just before adding to a dish to release the spicy scent. Grinding peppercorns in advance causes the perfume to fade. Instead of heat and scent, you are left with just a burning sensation.

Freshly ground black pepper has its own special, evocative perfume. *Don't* automatically add it to everything. Decide first if you want the qualities it offers in a dish. You may prefer a different spice aroma—or you may not want any spice at all.

buy in bulk

Natural food stores may seem more expensive but buying in bulk offers you tremendous savings. Collect a number of jars in different sizes, such as mason jars, which range from very small to very large.

Fill the jars with organic lentils, organic unbleached flour, organic beans, rice, sea salt, and spices. A good natural food store will expand your horizons immeasurably as you ponder which fragrant rice to select—or which bean from a colorful assortment that looks like candy in a candy shop. Dried spices bought in bulk cost a fraction of the price in supermarkets, which charge a hefty fee for packaging.

transitions: from bottled to bulk spices

Take a good, hard look in your spice cabinet. If you know which spices have been lingering in the dark way too long, ruthlessly dump them in the trash. Wash the spice jars and remove the labels. Dry bottle well, letting them air out completely.

Buy a fresh supply of each spice from a natural food store that has an active clientele; select spices from the section that sells them in bulk. You will get the freshest possible spices at a fraction of the cost of bottled ones. Buy small amounts and renew frequently.

Back home, transfer the spices to the empty spice jars; label them carefully (this is very important, since many are similar in appearance) and date each one before returning it to the darkness. Do not keep the spices longer than 6 months for optimum flavor.

canned tomatoes, organic or imported italian

During the months when fresh tomatoes are pale imitations of full summer fruit, I rely on high-quality canned tomatoes to make a tomato sauce. I would never think of making a fresh tomato sauce at any other time but summer.

Do not buy canned tomatoes that contain citric acids and firming agents. These tomatoes will produce sour sauces that must cook practically indefinitely to break down into a lightly textured puree. This long cooking destroys any fresh, juicy tomato qualities, and produces instead a heavy sauce with a distorted flavor.

Look for high-quality canned tomatoes that contain only salt, such as Italian San Marzano tomatoes or domestic organic tomatoes. With either, you can produce a miraculously fresh-tasting sauce that requires only a bare minimum of cooking.

fresh lemons

Always have lots of fresh lemons in the house. They are indispensable in my kitchen. I couldn't cook without them!

Both Eureka and Meyer lemons are good, but Meyer lemons are highly perfumed and less acidic. They are my personal favorites.

My supply comes from my mother's tree. When she visits me, she brings bags full to bursting with the deep golden fruits. Backyard gardens in citrus-producing climates often contain a Meyer lemon tree. And, fortunately, these delightful lemons are beginning to be sold in specialty produce markets.

garlic and onions, selecting and storing

Select garlic and onions that are firm to the touch, without soft spots and with no black areas between the skins.

Store garlic and onions in a dry and airy place.

Check each onion and garlic clove carefully before committing it to a dish.

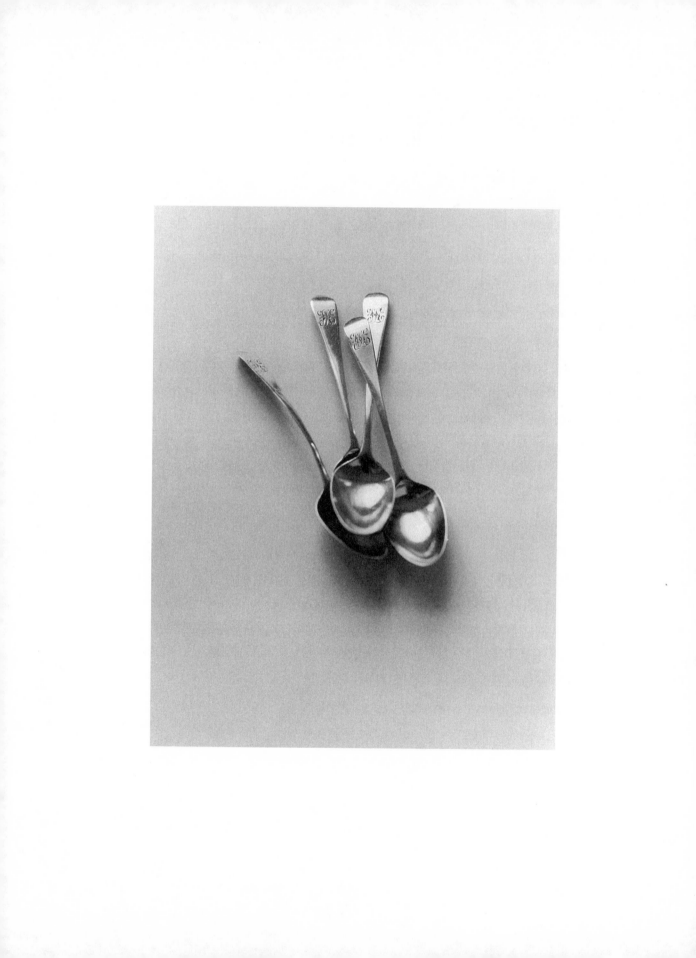

Andolina, Paola. *Cucina di Sicilia*. Palermo: Dario Flaccovio Editore, 1990.

Boni, Ada. *Italian Regional Cooking*. Bonanza Books, 1969.

Bradshaw, George, and Ruth Norman. *Cook Until Done*. New York: M. Barrows
and Company, 1962.

Callahan, Genevieve A. *Sunset All Western Foods*. San Francisco: Lane Publishing, 1947.

Carnacina, Luigi, and Luigi Veronelli. *La Cucina Rustica Regionale, 1. Italia Settentrionale*.
Milano: Rizzoli Editore, 1966.

Clark, Robert, editor. *Our Sustainable Table*. North Point Press, 1990.

Corey, Helen. *The Art of Syrian Cooking*. Garden City, N.Y.: Doubleday and Company,
Inc., 1962.

David, Elizabeth. All of her books.

Dolci, Danilo. *Sicilian Lives*. New York: Pantheon Books, 1981.

Editors of House and Garden. *House and Garden's New Cook Book*. New York:
The Conde Nast Publications, Inc., 1956.

Fisher, M.F.K. All of her books.

Fitzgerald, Dorothy. *The Quality Cook Book*. New York: Grosset and Dunlap, 1932.

Given, Meta. *The Modern Family Cookbook*. Chicago: J. G. Ferguson and Associates, 1942.

Gosetti, Fernanda. *Il Nuovo Orto in Tavola*. Milano: Arnoldo Mondadori Editore, 1988.

Harris, Valentina. *Regional Italian Cooking*. London: Walker Books, 1986.

Jones, Idwal. *Chef's Holiday*. New York, London, Toronto: Longmans, Green and
Company, Inc., 1952.

Karaoglan, Aida. *Food for the Vegetarian, Traditional Lebanese Recipes*. New York:
Interlink Books, 1988.

Lord Westbury and Donald Downes. *With Gusto and Relish*. London: Andre Deutsch,
Ltd., 1957.

Loren, Sophia. *In Cucina con Amore*. Milano: Rizzoli Editore, 1971.

McKenzie Hill, Janet. *Salads, Sandwiches and Chafing Dish Dainties*. Boston: Little, Brown,
and Company, 1899.

Bibliography

Mazza, Irma Goodrich. *Herbs for the Kitchen*. Boston: Little, Brown, and Company, 1939.

Mességué, Maurice. *C'est la Nature Qui a Raison*. Paris: Opera Mundi, 1972; American edition, *Maurice Mességué's Way to Natural Health and Beauty*. New York: Macmillan Publishing, 1974.

Olney, Richard. *The French Menu Cookbook*. New York: Simon and Schuster, 1970.

Olney, Richard. *Simple French Food*. New York: Atheneum, 1974, 1977.

Pepe, Antonietta. *Le Ricette della Mia Cucina Pugliese*. Firenze: Edizioni del Riccio, 1981.

Romagnoli, Margaret, and G. Franco. *The Romagnolis' Meatless Cookbook*. Boston and Toronto: Little, Brown, and Company, 1976.

Shircliffe, Arnold. *The Edgewater Beach Hotel Salad Book*. Chicago: American Hotel Register Company, Book Department, 1926.

Simonetta. *A Snob in the Kitchen*. Garden City, N.Y.: Doubleday and Company, Inc., 1967.

Smith, Herman. *Stina*. M. Barrows and Company, Inc., 1942.

Sorce, Rose. *The Complete Italian Cookbook*. New York: Grosset and Dunlap, 1953.

Toklas, Alice B. *The Alice B. Toklas Cookbook*. New York: Harper and Brothers, 1954.

Wason, Betty. *The Art of Vegetarian Cookery*. Garden City, N.Y.: Doubleday and Company, Inc., 1965.

Wechsberg, Joseph. *Blue Trout and Black Truffles*. New York: Alfred A. Knopf, Inc., 1953.

Index